PREACHING ON
DEVOTIONAL OCCASIONS

Other Mowbray Sermon Outlines
Series Editor: D. W. Cleverley Ford

PREACHING ON DEVOTIONAL OCCASIONS

D. W. Cleverley Ford

MOWBRAY
LONDON & OXFORD

Copyright © A. R. Mowbray & Co. Ltd 1986

ISBN 0 264 67044 2

First published 1986
by A. R. Mowbray & Co. Ltd,
Saint Thomas House, Becket Street,
Oxford, OX1 1SJ

Typeset by Acorn Bookwork, Salisbury, Wiltshire.
Printed in Great Britain by
Biddles Ltd, Guildford

British Library Cataloguing in Publication Data

Cleverley Ford, D. W.
    Preaching on devotional occasions. – (Mowbray's
sermon outlines)
    1. Sermons – Outlines, syllabi, etc.
    I. Title
    251'.02   BV4223

    ISBN 0-264-67044-2

CONTENTS

ACKNOWLEDGEMENTS

I wish to thank the Publishing Division of Messrs A. R. Mowbray & Co. Ltd for inviting me to write this book, and also
those who have asked me to address various audiences on
devotional occasions so causing much of the material for it to
be worked out. And to Miss Barbara Hodge of Canterbury I
am indebted for putting her professional expertise into the
production of an attractive typewritten text for the printers.

An extract from 'Surgical Ward' from *Collected Poems* by
W. H. Auden is reproduced by permission of Faber and Faber
Limited.

Lingfield 1985   D. W. CLEVERLEY FORD

INTRODUCTION

Sunday worship is the context in which the ministry of preaching is for the most part carried out. It would be a mistake however to reckon that this provides the only occasion. There are others. There are week-day meetings, notably in Lent, and there are quiet days, retreats and conferences when devotional themes are most frequently handled. It is to help with these that this book has been written.

On these occasions it is not uncommon for the spoken word to be called 'an address' and not a sermon, though precisely what is the difference is not clear. Perhaps 'address' sounds less pompous. There is, however, a difference in most of the addresses in this book from what would be provided for sermons in the course of liturgical worship, in that they are rather longer. The reason is obvious. Partakers settling down for a quiet day will not have their expectations met with three homilies of seven minutes' duration each. They have come for the day. Moreover they will expect some substance, something to mull over during the silent periods which should form a part of every quiet day. What is more, because the occasion is special, those who have made the effort to be present are a little special in themselves, perhaps more than a little. They can 'take in' more than the average member of the average Sunday congregation. Be prepared then, in this book, for material fairly tightly packed in some places, but not, I trust, heavy.

Be prepared also for variety in style. This is demanded by the nature of the occasion, a fact more readily appreciated if I reveal where some of the addresses have been given. The Good Friday addresses formed part of a series of seven delivered to a large congregation in the large church of St Peter Mancroft in Norwich. They could not be quietly spoken. They had to be proclaimed. The Holy Week addresses on the other hand were given to a small congregation in one of the chapels in the cathedral from a chair in front of the altar. They were styled accordingly. The three quiet day addresses were given at a course for prospective ordinands, readers and lay preachers (the latter in Churches other than Anglican) arranged by the Chaplains' Department of the Royal Navy and the Royal Air Force at Amport House, Andover. The course on leadership at the end of the book was provided for a much smaller group still – diocesan leaders in Liverpool. Addresses At Compline have to be very short indeed, containing only one major thought. Work done for the Southwark Ordination Course forms the basis for some of these.

Once again, in this book as in others of mine, I have not missed out the personal or topical allusions. Sermons or addresses often fail to reach people when these are absent, simply because they are impersonal. There is a danger of course that the preacher/speaker will indulge in an ego-trip, fatal for him and for his audience. Nevertheless sermons and addresses that are wholly abstract do not belong anywhere, and sermons and addresses should always belong. I cannot refrain from saying, even with my tongue in my cheek, that if I leave in these personal and topical allusions no one will be able to reproduce them just as they stand! No one is meant even to try! The hope is rather that not only preachers but also readers of this book who are not preachers and never will be preachers, will be stimulated devotionally by what they find so that the attention given will in itself constitute a *devotional occasion*, perhaps even an extension of a spoken ministry that has already taken place.

D.W.C.F.

ADVENT MEDITATIONS

1 What God is like

1 *Our world without Christmas*

I want to begin our devotional preparation for Christmas with what you may consider a ridiculous idea! I want to begin by inviting you to try and imagine our thoughts and feelings if Christmas did not exist at all. Now, like you, I could laugh this off. I could say 'Good, no more of those Christmas cards to select; no more of that mind-searching anxiety about whom we may have inadvertently left off our list – Aunt Agatha, for instance, whom we haven't seen for years but who would be really upset if she did not receive an annual picture of a robin in the snow; no more of that exhausting shopping expedition to try to find suitable presents for eighteen grandchildren, just as if we could know what is suitable. Pity about the office party, of course, but even that raises problems.' So not more than one tear perhaps, or even two, if Christmas were no more.

But wait a minute. Let us be serious. Very well, you say; it would be a pity not to have a season of goodwill at the close of each year. God knows, there is enough strife in the world these days. You can scarcely open the newspaper, or turn on television without learning of someone's head bashed in, or a whole tribe starved to death. Yes, let us be reminded for a day or two at least in December of how happiness comes from co-operating with people and not forever fighting with people. All right, Christmas is sentimental, but where have scientific calculations, logic and rationalism by themselves taken us? No, on second thoughts our world really would be empty without Christmas.

2 *What is God like?*

And now I am going to risk being 'heavy' and come in with an encouragement to dig deeper; indeed if I didn't I can't really see much point in my preaching at all as a preparation for Christmas. After all you don't need my help in how to organ-

1

ize a party, or which presents are suitable for 'teenagers'. What I wish to say is that Christmas tells us *what God is like*. And you think that pretty commonplace, the sort of remark a clergyman is supposed to make in the pulpit. But is it commonplace?

What *is* God like? You tell me. Go and stand outside on one of these starlit winter nights, look up at the galaxies in the sky and know that you can see only one galaxy of all the galaxies on galaxies that exist. And read what the astronomers tell us about the immensity of space, and their theories how it all began with a big bang – but what caused the bang? There must have been something there already to bang, so the theory tells us nothing about the origins of the universe. We just don't know. Nor does it tell us what God is like. Or listen to the biologists. They work with a theory of evolution, admittedly only a theory, but we should be rather silly to try and refute it. We can be reasonably sure that the physical world as we know it has developed gradually over millions of years. So what does this tell us about God? Very little.

And then you take up the newspaper, or some recent history book, let alone an ancient one, and learn of the catastrophes that have followed for some people as a result of devastating floods, droughts, earthquakes, and the ravages of plagues of locusts. I repeat my question – What is God like? I do not say, Is there a God? because reasoning on the basis of scientific fact is quite as capable of pointing in the direction of belief in God as refuting it. I am asking about the *nature* of God, to be deduced from our observation of it, conditioned as we are in the Western world by scientific modes of thinking which cannot be bypassed or jettisoned. From looking at the world God created and continuously creates through the processes of nature what would you say he is like?

3 *Man is the clue*

My guess is – this question will stump you. And for this reason, that everything in the physical world works strictly according *to its own nature*. Fire burns. Water drowns. Rocks on the Alps come crashing down when the sun in spring melts the glaciers, completely without respect of climbers or cafés. Even your beautiful domestic cat will tear to pieces that lovely blue tit feeding on the coconut you have set out for its feed. Such is the cat's nature. Everything in God's world works according to its intrinsic nature without any other considerations. It cannot do otherwise.

There is however, *one exception*, just one, and that exception is the human being, also created by God. A human being does not only function according to his/her nature. Other consider-ations (yes, *considerations* implying mind), enter in as motives of prudence, justice and love. Here then is the place to look for the clue as to what God is like – in the human being, imperfect no doubt, but pointing the way to the nature of God as nothing else in the created order can.

4 *God assumed flesh*

And so I come to Christmas. And perhaps you are saying, Thank heaven, all this abstract reasoning is really too much. But I haven't quite finished. If God has set in this world men able to give the clue as to what God is like, is it not reasonable to think that since men and women, for all their expertise make such a sorry show, and can even remind us at times more of the devil than of God – is it not reasonable to think that God should at least show us what he himself is like *in a perfect man*?

And this is what Christmas is really about, only you have to dig deep in order to appreciate it. In Jesus, yes, beginning with the baby Jesus in the manger the eternal Word of God took on human flesh – the theological word is 'incarnate', becoming a man and walking about in our world. Ordinary people going about their ordinary lives saw him and actually touched him. Mary his mother touched him. She washed him, fed him and cuddled him. And he developed into a man people found to be quite remarkable. I believe, and not without reason, that we have a shallow religion unless we accept that this man, Jesus of Nazareth, is the Word of God, telling us what God is like. Is not this what St John says in his gospel which we read every Christmas – *So the Word became flesh; he*

*came to dwell among us, and we saw his glory, such glory as befits the
Father's only Son, full of grace and truth.* (John 1.14)

So this is what I am saying in our Advent preparation for
Christmas. The physical world, the world of nature (if you
like) does show us a part of God's working (philosophers
would say 'thinking'); but to what God is *in himself*, what is his
nature, what he is like, only man, only human beings can give
the clue, for we are all made in the likeness of God, and the *full
likeness* is in Jesus Christ, so full that what can we do but bow
the knee?

> *'Thou art the King of glory: O Christ.*
> *Thou art the everlasting Son: of the Father.'*

We must start here.

PRAYER

> *Lord Jesus Christ*
> *You have come to us*
> *To help us see —*
>> *See What God is like,*
>> *See What God has done,*
>> *See what God will do,*
> *For those who trust him.*
> *Help us Lord to see.*

2 Where God meets us

> Matthew 1.12, 15, 16 (NEB) *Jeconiah was
> the father of Shealtiel ... Eleazar of Matthan,
> Matthan of Jacob, Jacob of Joseph, the husband
> of Mary, who gave birth to Jesus called Messiah.*

I would like you to imagine that you are sitting at home one
night when the door bell rings. You hesitate to answer it.
When you do you are on your guard. A stranger is standing

there. You know nothing about him. He might even be a foreigner. Clearly he is outside your circle of acquaintances and friends. You move to close the door, but he steps nearer. 'Don't you know me?' he asks. 'I am your brother.' All at once the yawning gap is closed. You and he are tied by an indissoluble bond, a blood bond. It could bring you the utmost joy. On the other hand it could fill you with the deepest dread and dismay. My brother! Oh!

1 *In family joys and tensions*

Christmas is a time for the family. There are joys in family life, fundamental joys but there are tensions too. Christmas may even sharpen them. It is a sad fact how marriage guidance counsellors report that after Christmas, when families have been together for days, there are more applications for help against breakdown than usual. Is it strange then that family life has something to tell us about God at Christmas time? But it has. God entered our world through a family. He might have come to us as an angel, or a voice, or a man with neither ancestry nor progeny like Melchizedek in the Bible; but no, he came through the gate of family life with its joys and its tensions.

Turgenev, the Russian novelist, has a story in his classic *Fathers and Sons* about an offensive man called Bazarov, the nihilist son of a pious old couple whose bitter disappointment over him never wholly quenched their love. All this is painfully mirrored in a final graveyard scene in a remote corner of Russia where he lay buried. Every so often this frail old couple could be seen supporting each other to the grave, walking with heavy steps. There, invariably, they fell on their knees by the iron railings weeping bitter tears. Then exchanging the briefest of words they dusted the stone which bore the son's name. Then they prayed. For a long time they knelt there unable to tear themselves away. They had drunk to the full the joy of family life but also to the depths its sour sorrows. . . . This was the gate through which God entered our world at Christmas, the gateway of the family.

We must of course be careful not to be so obsessed with the tensions that we forget the joys, even the hilarious times. There is fun in a family even if the boys do engage in pillow fights, the girls pull each other's hair, and the boys put frogs in their sisters' beds. Nor must we reckon that Jesus stood outside this fun. He knew it and laughed with it, and I guess took part in it, making his own contribution. But he also knew the tension. Think what lies behind the statement in the fourth gospel that his brothers did not believe in him! Imagine the snide remarks! Picture the pain in Mary's, the mother's eyes.

What does this tell us about God? What does it say to a girl who is miserable at home? What does it say to those in a broken home? Has it any message for people suffering the petty jealousies and rivalries that spoil wider family circles, and some who even help to cause them? Are situations like these, and the people mixed up in them, completely outside any possibility of God making himself known there? No doubt we can accommodate our minds to the idea of men and women crying to God for mercy in the terrifying major catastrophes of war, famine and pestilence, but what about the nagging little domestic fracas and misunderstandings which, for all their triviality, little by little lay low the men and women who have to live with them? Who wants to talk about these tensions? Who is not half ashamed of them? We reckon God is far too transcendent for this sort of littleness. He cannot possibly stoop to such levels as these. Are you sure? Does not Christmas come back year after year to remind us that God in Christ entered our world through the little gateway of a little family where he grew up with four brothers and at least two sisters? God understands. God is concerned. We can pray to God about the trivial tensions of which we are half ashamed. That resentful mood of mine last week. That outburst of jealousy I ought to have kept to myself. And if we come to God in prayer about the trivialities, always remembering to preface our prayer with praises, for we have much for which to be thankful – most of us – in our families, who knows but that we may not grow in personal stature and maturity right there? Home is the place where we can grow up in more ways than physically. Jesus did this.

6

And now a second observation. We can choose our friends but not our relations. Families *find* themselves together. Sometimes we talk about a family network. A network can trap as it does with fish at sea. To struggle free is exceedingly difficult, if not impossible. So with a family. One member by his actions can disgrace not only himself but his whole family. It is not all that rare for people to be obliged to change their name because a brother or sister, parent or uncle has so blackened the family name that it is impossible to live with it any longer. I do not know if there are any men or women around now belonging to the families of Göring and Goebbels, but if so they could not continue with those nefarious names.

The truth is we may be ashamed of our families. The equal truth is that we may be proud of our families. Perhaps to grasp at first how we may be netted by some disgrace in our families is easier than to see how we may be netted by pride in our families. Family pride can, and often does, tar people with an unattractive *hauteur*, the ordinary word for which is snobbery. It is impossible for all but the equally privileged to come near to these people. They live in a supposed superior world apart, though as often as not there are sharp inter-family rivalries within that world. It is not wrong however to be proud of our families. It is certainly right to respect the family which possesses a long and impressive ancestry. A family which has kept itself intact down the centuries has achieved something of real value.

Whichever way you look at it then, the family can act as a net which ensnares. All the more surprising then that when God created our world he came right into this net. Look at chapter 1 of St Matthew's gospel. There you will see a long family tree for Jesus. Look at Luke, chapter 3, and you will see another. Yes, I know they are artificially constructed and the two do not exactly tally. I am sufficient of a New Testament scholar to be aware of this. But what are the authors saying by including these genealogies in their narratives? What are they seeking to proclaim about God's entry into our world? Surely that he came so close in it that he was *netted in a family* as we are netted, and yet he lived as Son of God. We ought to 'take in' the fact of these family trees in the gospels of St Matthew and St Luke, for they are the same two gospels, the only two, which record the virgin birth. It is as if the writers were saying, Yes, the virgin birth can be made to look as if Jesus was free of the family limitations that must accompany the entry of all of us into the world; but it wasn't so; he had a long ancestry, some of it distinguished, of which he would be proud, some of it poor and mean, of which he would be ashamed. Jesus was not, however, netted by this network of his family background which was chosen for him. He rose above it, became out of it, and because of it, what he was.

To honour the family and yet not to be netted by the family, this is the call to every Christian man and woman.

3 *In the challenge of heredity*

Now this. A lesson not infrequently drawn from the Christmas story is how great and good people sometimes derive from apparently hopelessly impoverished circumstances. Jesus was cradled in a manger in someone's stable yard. What chance, you say. The conditions in which we are brought up are responsible for the kind of people we turn out to be. How hard our social reformers have driven this point home, and with some justification. Even so, the environment is not the sole governing factor determining what we are. Jesus was reared up some dingy alleyway in the pokey town of Nazareth.

The other factor said to condition what we turn out to be is heredity, and, like environment, it cannot be discounted. Similarly it cannot be made to necessitate the kind of people we are. Balzac, the French novelist, fascinated by the ins and outs of family life tells a story in his book *La Cousine Bette* of one called Baron Hûlot in Paris about 1840 – an inveterate womanizer. You wonder however an intelligent man could be caught time and time again by the pretty faces of his expensive Parisian mistresses till they had filched all the money out of his considerable pockets, bringing him down to the gutter. What chance, you think, for the children of such a rake? But the son became an honourable lawyer and the daughter made the best

8

of an unsuitable marriage. No, sometimes sons and daughters achieve success by reacting *against* their forbears. I have seen it happen. Heredity does not have the final word in what we become. We cannot excuse ourselves so easily. Not only that Jesus issued from a cramped environment, he had heredity to contend with as we have. Not all his forbears were oil paintings.

So from within the network of the family, circumstances and heredity, God comes to us where we are. Each one is called to rise to the height of his own, her own, individuality. We need not be trapped. Jesus was not trapped. We need not run away because of our family. We ought not to 'take it easy', either, because of our family of which we may be justly proud. Our Christmas gospel, I was going to say our 'Christian gospel' recognizes a dignity in every man and woman. Let us hear the word of God and rise to its challenge. Through this response comes fulness of life, and what joy and satisfaction it contains.

PRAYER

> Almighty God our Father,
> from whom every family in heaven and on earth is named,
> we thank you for our families and forbears
> most of whom we have never known.
> Give us grace to build on the good we have received
> and to shun the mediocre that has come down to us.
> May we develop the individuality which is ours by right
> destined at the last to be conformed to the image of Jesus Christ,
> our liberator and enabler.

3 How God surprises us

> Luke 1.11 (RSV) *And there appeared to him an angel of the Lord standing on the right side of the altar of incense.*

I wonder if you have ever been given the money at Christmas to go out and buy your own Christmas present. Maybe with good reason. The donor was ill or absent abroad. Whatever the reason, this I can guess at – you felt flat buying your own present. The truth is, we like our presents to be surprises. We even like negotiating those sellotaped parcels apparently designed to take the time up to the Christmas following to unstick them, they are so tightly wrapped. I can tell you why we like them, because they contain surprises. We do not know what is inside.

Christmas to be Christmas needs to contain surprises. It needs to contain surprises if it is to be in line with the New Testament presentation of Christmas. The Christmas and pre-Christmas stories in the gospels of St Matthew and St Luke are full of surprises. I expect they are told in this way to teach us that unless we reckon with surprise we cannot really enter into the Christian experience of God.

(A) *Preparation for surprises*

Let us start with St Luke's pre-Christmas story. It begins with a dull picture, but if you want to reinforce a bright light you set it against a dark background. So here is an old couple who are almost too good to be true. Never once have they stepped out of the orthodox line. And their pedigree was spotless. Back and back you could go and trace their ultra-respectable ancestry. And there were no children of this marriage. No one after them to get up to any pranks. No wayward sons or daughters to break out of the uniform family pattern. Here was dullness with no sign of any lifting of the greyness. Even the husband's way of ministering at the altar of incense in the temple itself was not unexpected. His name was simply listed there in the official rota, obtainable no doubt from the temple information office. But he was in for a surprise, a fantastic surprise – there appeared to him an angel of the Lord, standing on the right side of the altar of incense!

Most of us do not reckon with angels in life, except possibly on Christmas cards. We don't really reckon with them in ecclesiastical circles, although we have set carvings of them on our church ceilings, painted in gold. I have to confess that

10

when I carry out my duty once a year in one of our cathedrals I never expect to see an angel on the right side of the altar, which only goes to show how I, too, need to take note of this Lucan story.

And now a second surprise. The angel promised this old couple a son. And that sounded ridiculous. Zechariah (that was the man's name) more or less told the angel so. What a way to answer an angel! It is reasonable to assume that there was nothing this couple had prayed for more earnestly than a child, but they had long since given up that prayer. After all, it is no use praying against nature. Well, is it? No intelligent person can reckon with surprises on that scale in religion. So maybe Zechariah was a latitudinarian by now!

And now a third surprise. Zechariah, having doubted the angel's promise of a son, found that he could not speak. Note this. Doubt produces dumbness. When we will not believe what God promises, we have nothing to say, nothing anyway that produces hope. This is the root problem about rationalism and why it so frequently fails to be creative of buoyant life. Not that all doubt is evil. A person who has never doubted is probably a person who has never really thought. Doubt can be an important tool for the advancement of knowledge. There is even a proper agnosticism. About some aspects of life it is right to say, 'we do not know'. Yet the truth still stands; if there is an unwillingness – that is the key word 'unwillingness' – to reckon with surprise in the Christian faith, we shall find that in the end we have no gospel to proclaim.

And now a fourth surprise. Contrary to the whole history of names in Zechariah's and Elizabeth's families, the angel said this child of promise was to be called John. And when the child was born and brought to the naming ceremony the family protestations were loud and clear. Zechariah however was obedient, the child received the name John. And if that was a surprise, it was nothing like the surprise when Zechariah began to speak once more; and even that paled before what he spoke, the canticle we know as the Benedictus. So the old priest suddenly became a prophet, and that too, was a surprise.

11

(B) *Surprises in human experience*

1 *Organized religion*

What has all this to say to us? Surely that we must be careful how we write off organized religion. You never know – an angel may appear. Not of course when you expect an appearance, more likely when you least expect it. If I may speak roughly for a moment – God has a way of catching us 'on the hop'. An angel will certainly not be standing there every time we enter a church to kneel for worship. Spiritual experience of this intense kind – and this is what is meant by an angelic appearance – is very rare. The general rule seems to be that we all have to manage with a mere handful of great moments in our spiritual pilgrimage, and for the greater part live in the memory of them. I do not read that even Mary the mother of Jesus had more than one initial angelic appearance. This, however, is paramount – we must be ready for surprises, even in routine religion.

Let me press this point. At the present time there is a certain weariness with organized religion. There are people ready to write off the local church as too boringly dull to be a possible cradle for any kind of vigorous life or thinking. Yet the New Testament tells us that out of such a milieu the Christian faith emerged. No doubt there are those who would be far happier to discover that the Christian movement originated in some radical 'think tank', or some social welfare conference; and some perhaps, among ascetics in a monastery; but no, its origins were in the routine of orthodox family piety.

So be careful how you write off your church. Vivid spiritual awareness can come through sung Eucharist in a cathedral. It can occur in 1662 Mattins. Evening worship with guitars in the local chapel, with hand clapping, may produce an angel for someone, even the BBC's *Songs of Praise* programmes. You never know. You never know when God will draw near with the reality of his presence. We must be ready for surprises.

2 *The call to faith*

And now this – never get over the surprise that God should have called you to faith in him. After all, why is it that you are a believer and the man, the woman, next door is not? They are no less intelligent. They are equally respectable. Can you honestly say that your faith is the outcome of your goodness? You know it is not. But here you are present at this devotional occasion. And I am leading it! And I do not come from a clerical family. Why am I a priest in the Church of England?

If you pick up Margaret Duggan's book, *The Making of an Archbishop* (1983), you will find that the parents of the present Archbishop of Canterbury were non-churchgoers. He went to a confirmation class with another boy because both were keen on the same girl, and she was attending the class.

The Christian life is full of surprises. If you can't bear surprises then have nothing to do with it, because we can never get the ways of God with us 'taped'. He will call whom he will, and from whatever circumstances he will. If this 'cuts us down to size' so be it. Christmas has much to do with humbling oneself.

3 *The call to service*

You may be called to service as a Christian man or woman. Don't be too surprised. But if you are, do not reckon you know how or where God will use you. I have seen a few called from upper class circles to work in the slums. I have seen some called from the humblest of circumstances to work in the corridors of power. You never know. My guess is that if Zechariah and Elizabeth had lived long enough to see their precious son grow up they would have wished that he wore some decent clothes and not that ugly rough coat of camel's hair, with a leather belt to keep it on. Far better, from the point of view of this tidy pair, that their son ministered in the temple in a decent alb and chasuble, or their equivalent. But the decision as to what God will make of those he calls does not lie with the called, least of all with their parents, but with God, who does the calling. So be ready for surprises should you be

13

called to service. The more certain the call the more certain the surprises. And do not limit the call to service to ordained service. There are lay ministries in lay situations. God has used housewives and farm workers before now to bring people to himself.

Conclusion

Christmas then tells us to be ready for surprises. Perhaps I should change the word and say, it tells us we should be ready for miracles. I know that is hard to take. After all, I too am a twentieth-century man conditioned by scientific modes of thinking. But this I have learnt, that if we are to have the religion of the New Testament at all we shall have to entertain the concept of miracle. This is why we can't offload the incarnation and the resurrection of Jesus. Which being so, what you and I can properly do is to kneel in wonder, love and praise, before the Christmas manger to renew our acceptance of the surprise gift of God's eternal life.

PRAYER

> *Lord you surprise us;*
> *You are always surprising us;*
> *You surprised us at Bethlehem,*
> *You surprised us at Calvary.*
> *Open our minds to surprises now,*
> *to surprises in your way with us.*
> *Nothing need be stereotyped,*
> *nothing impossible,*
> *because everything is in your hand,*
> *the God of surprises.*

4 What Mary gave to Jesus

Luke 1.38 (AV) *And Mary said, Behold the handmaid of the Lord; be it unto me according to thy word.*

1 *Jesus's mother*

Jesus must have had a mother. Of this fact we can be sure. There are people, of course, and genuine Christians among them, who assert that he must have possessed a father as well; but this is not what the Scriptures say. They tell us he was born of the Virgin Mary his mother who came to be with child of the Holy Spirit. Not that those who reject the virgin birth necessarily deny the incarnation of God in Christ, they even suggest that God came closer to us if Jesus was conceived as we are conceived, that is, with both father and mother. Their view then of these nativity stories brought to our attention every Christmas in that way are pictorial creations of what came to be believed about Jesus after his resurrection, that he was the eternal Son of God. They are theology in story form.

Some of you may consider what I am saying an odd way to begin an address on a devotional occasion such as this; and I must confess it almost goes against the grain for me too, because I want to get on and think with you about Jesus's mother and what she gave him. If however I do not show myself aware of the modern critical approach to these Christmas stories, of which you too, may be aware from some RE course you have taken, or from some radio broadcasts you have heard; and also if I do not make clear at the outset that I am not prepared to un-Church those Christians who cannot 'take' the virgin birth (though I accept it myself) – I repeat, if I do not make clear both these points at the outset – blockage will remain, making it difficult, if not impossible, for you to hear any word of God from these scriptures about the nativity, and this above all is what I should like us to hear.

2 *Jesus received from his mother*

Jesus must have had a mother. No one can gainsay this. And he must have received from his mother physical characteris-

15

tics, such as Jewish features, the timbre of his voice, even some mannerisms. No one looked like Jesus and sounded like Jesus so much as his mother. He must also have received from her character traits as well. All of which must mean that if we owe anything to Jesus as a man we must owe something to his mother who bore him. And the more we come to adore the man so much the more are we bound to set the mother on a pinnacle by herself. So the statement in Luke 1.42 is not excessive, *Blessed art thou among women*.

And now suppose we 'take in' what is most likely, that Mary was only about fourteen when she gave him birth. Hans Küng, in his book, *Eternal Life?* published in Germany in 1982, and in England in 1984, tells us that the average length of life for a man now in Germany, and presumably in other Western lands, is 70, for a woman 75. In 1876, that is a hundred years ago, it was 34, and in the time of Jesus and of the Roman emperors, people rarely lived beyond the age of 20. So Jesus beginning his ministry at about 30 was exceptional, and his mother watching by the Cross at the end would have been even more exceptional, for she must have been at least 45.

Since Mary then was such a young mother what could she give her child beyond physical characteristics? We must face this. One of the facts of life however is that motherhood has a way of deepening women almost overnight. I saw this for myself over a period of seven years in a situation far removed from that of Mary. It was a home (so-called) in my first parish run by the diocesan authority for unmarried mothers. I visited that home every Wednesday and I must confess it strained my powers of conversation to the limits. If they were not bad girls they were certainly utterly silly and painfully shallow. But invariably as soon as their child was born they were open to reasonable conversation and discussion. The transformation brought about by motherhood was quite remarkable. If this could happen with these girls, how much more a thousand times with Mary. Yes, Jesus certainly received from his mother. There was much to receive.

What could, what did Mary give to child Jesus? I want to suggest three priceless gifts. I shall have to list them and deal with them separately, but this is not how they were given. They were imparted together and because they were imparted together in the unification of personal contact of mother and child they were wholesome and wholemaking. Each in isolation could make for an imbalance, which is unwholesome. I stress this personal contact. Mary being so young a mother, the distance in years between her and Jesus was reduced to a minimum. To put the matter another way. Mother and child were very close. They would play happily together and he would learn quickly from her, the intimacy of the one-roomed house where they undoubtedly lived accentuating the closeness. What did Jesus learn from Mary?

(a) Discipline

Discipline was certainly something he learnt, something she gave him. At the most elementary level of all, the control of his natural functions, but much more than that. This was a Jewish household, and Jewish life, down to the last detail, was regulated by what is called the Torah, the Law. The discipline extended to food, clothes, washing, neighbourliness, business, worshipping, praying, even to thinking. There was no part of life to which the Law did not apply. So much was Jewish life regulated that the surrounding nations looked on with amazement. The fact cannot be gainsaid that the heights of achievement which have always been a characteristic of the Jewish people stem in no small part from the discipline imparted to them from infancy. After all, there is no excellence in any part of life able to be achieved without the routine of disciplined practice. Discipline requires the conquest of moods and appetites. People who cannot master themselves, and this includes their tongues, will not master life. The Christian Church has its ordered life. There are seasons to be kept, Lent is perhaps one of the best known, and keeping it, like all routines, can be deadly if recognized merely as an end in itself, even contributing to spiritual pride; but if it is used to

17

achieve and retain personal mastery, it acts as the key to achievement. It was not by accident that Jesus was accorded the title 'Master' in later years, master of his powers, master of his speech, master of his fears. Discipline was Mary's gift to him, the gift of her ordered home. And if we profess to follow him it is right to enquire what discipline we exercise in our own Christian profession. Are we disciplined people?

(b) Trust

Another priceless gift Mary gave Jesus was trust. This is summed up in what is one of the most significant sayings in the gospels on the lips of anyone apart from Jesus himself. It occurs in that passage of scripture we call the annunciation, in Luke chapter 1, verses 26–38, when Mary was made aware that she was to become the mother of him whom we have come to know as the saviour of the world, achieving his ministry by way of rejection and death. *Be it unto me according to thy word.* Trust was required from her. There would be joy at his birth. There is invariably joy at a birth, birth of a first-born son. There would be deep satisfaction at his remarkable development; but there would be pain too. There always is with a child growing into adolescence and manhood. A gap develops. Independence has to be won and kept. Mary felt all this and it hurt. The indications are plain enough in the gospel records for all to see, and for mothers especially, to feel. Yet for all the pain, experienced and expected, Mary trusted God. There was no rebellion. She was willing to do her heavenly Father's will. And it sustained her even through the crucifixion scene. That trust, that unwavering trust, seeped into Jesus with his mother's milk. He never departed from it by a hair's breadth, indeed, it became the mainspring of his utterly unique ministry. Which of us has trusted God like Jesus? Which like Mary his mother? But we cannot deny that the pattern for us is here.

(c) Love

And of course Mary gave her child Jesus love. It is natural for a mother to love her child. Properly speaking a child is the product of love. No child can certainly develop in a wholesome fashion without love. There has to be an atmosphere of love.

18

There has to be a place where love is felt. A home where the love of the parents for each other is not obvious is a poor place for the nurture and welfare of children. And they must be sure of it. They must not doubt it. They must take it for granted. Do not miss the point, Jesus in part came to be what we know him to be because Mary loved him. Mother's love can of course be possessive, and Mary had to learn the hard lesson of having that kind of love broken. She had to let Jesus, when he became a man, go his way, which was not her way, and still to love him. Intelligent love, not sentimental love is the love that enriches. Mary was intelligent, or how could anyone ever think of putting the words of the Magnificat into her mouth, even if she did not compose them all herself, modelling them on the song of Hannah in the Hebrew scriptures she knew so well? There is hardly anything more influential in this world than the love of a wise woman, an intelligent (which does not mean erudite or clever) mother. It was with this that Jesus was blessed. None of us can choose our mothers, but we can learn from Mary the mother of Jesus what is the nature of the kind of love that is a priceless gift.

Conclusion

What has all this to say to us in preparation for Christmas? Surely this, that homes before anything else are the training grounds for character because only there do the priceless gifts of discipline, trust and love come in a personal context. And in all this, the key figure is the mother.

Lord Jesus Christ,
You had a mother
 a disciplined mother
 a trusting mother
 a mother who loved deeply.
And because the whole Christian Church is in you by faith,
 somehow your mother is our mother.
  We reverence her.
  We praise her.
  We learn from her
 what a mother can give her child,
 what women can give to mankind,
 what resources there are in women
 that your early training was entrusted to a woman.
We thank you, Lord, for Mary,
  and for all that women have given us,
  in the name of Jesus Christ,
   Mary's son,
   our Lord.

LENTEN ADDRESSES

Let us confess our sins in penitence and
faith firmly resolved to keep God's commandments and to live in love and peace
with all men.
(*ASB The Order for Holy Communion Rite A*
Section 26, p. 127)

1 Confessing our sins

Hebrews 12.1 (NEB) *We must throw off every
encumbrance, every sin to which we cling.*

You will not be surprised that I have chosen to speak today
about sins. Indeed, to keep Ash Wednesday, the first day of
Lent, without speaking about sins, gloomy as it may sound,
would be to fly in the face of the Christian tradition. But I do
not want to be gloomy. This is why I have decided to handle
this subject under the title, 'Confessing our sins'. What concerns the Christian gospel is not harping on our sins which can
be morbid, nor is it dissembling or cloaking them, as the Book
of Common Prayer puts it. Both are bad reactions. Our concern is to recognize our sins as encumbrances in the race of life
to which everyone is committed and then to throw them off so
as to run with confidence and efficiency, a song in our hearts.

1 *Missing the mark*

When I put the matter this way you will see that I am not
visualizing sins as the breaking of external rules of behaviour
but as hindrances to personal fulfilment. What I hear God
saying today, Ash Wednesday, is this. You would be a better
man, a better woman, and so would I, if we faced up to the
things that drag us down. This is not the only way sin is
understood in the Bible, but it is one way, and I think a
helpful way for people like ourselves sensitive enough about
our spiritual condition to attend a devotional occasion such as

21

this. So understood, sin is represented in the New Testament by the Greek word *hamartia*, which means missing the mark. The picture is of an archer with a splendid quiverful of arrows polished and pointed; but he does not hit the target as he should and could, his shots are often way out and he knows it. Similarly sin is not living up to our own ideals. We fall short too often of our own best.

Many years ago I had a friend, who has since died, for whom I had a considerable regard. He possessed a brilliant mind and I learned much from his acuteness. He never, however, achieved in his life the high position of which he was capable. There was, I fear, an element of sloth in him which he seemed unable to shake off. He had excellent university degrees and one further high qualification lay within his grasp if only he would complete the thesis he had in mind. But he wouldn't 'get down to it', as we say. He was always going to begin tomorrow, and tomorrow never came. All those years ago I was sorry to see that weakness in him. Not that his life turned out to be a failure but I think he did miss his mark. He could have done more, much more.

2 *Specific encumbrances*

What are some of the encumbrances which hinder us in running effectively the race that is set before us?

High up in the list I place *resentment* at the deal we have received in life. To put this round the other way, I believe it is imperative to accept the way life happens to have come to us. I can't explain how it is or why it should be that this girl is born with a cleft palate and that boy with one leg shorter than the other. I recognize the frustration of poverty and the pain of living in a broken home. We don't all begin on the same scratch line, some begin behind it. Others have an enormous start. It is not always an advantage to possess a brilliant and famous father; sometimes the son suffers a deep sense of inferiority in consequence, but he is at least noticed, he doesn't have to fight for recognition. This is the point. If we resent the pack of cards life has dealt out to us, we shall not be able to make much use of them at all. Accepting our circumstances does not mean sitting down under them. That MP for Cardiff West we heard of the other day, Stephan Terlezki, who somehow arrived in this country after the war penniless and alone, having escaped from the slave labour camps in Austria where he was thrust as a boy of fifteen by Hitler's armies invading the Ukraine, must have cast resentment at his lot overboard very very soon or he would never have achieved what he has. Acceptance is not resignation. It is casting off resentment and making the best use of what we have. Ash Wednesday calls us to this and it extends even to that rainy day we so dislike.

And now *depression*. It is so easy I know to be depressed these days as a result of the news bulletins. And there are personal setbacks, failures and disappointments for us all, not least on account of our missing the mark we know we ought to hit. Maybe medical help is necessary for some with a depressive illness, or the assistance of some pastoral counsellor. Fair enough, but ordinary, everyday depression can be thrown off. I once had a secretary who used to say that she thought it quite wrong to off-load on to other people, especially those living close to us, our own personal problems by being depressed. For others' sake, she insisted, we have a duty to be cheerful. And she was, without being exuberant which can be tiresome. It is better to tell someone what is worrying rather than to bear it alone in depression. Depression often lifts by sharing the worry. Be that as it may, depression must be fought in its initial stages before it obtains a hold, otherwise to dislodge it is difficult and the result is a depressed person one is tempted to avoid.

Another encumbrance is *criticism of other people*. There is a sense, of course, in which it has to be. Some of us have had that frightening responsibility of having to sit on selection boards, as they are called, even to chair them and make the final decision. In those situations it is essential that the various candidates applying for the job in question should be summed up. Strengths and weaknesses have to be noted. And in another situation altogether, God help the girl who cannot judge the character of the man who is running after her. In this sense we have to be critical of people, but it does not mean we condemn them. Who knows how we should have fared had we been dealt the pack of cards dealt by life to them? There is a warning here which may be particularly necessary in church circles. Gossip and tittle-tattle are an encumbrance to the

23

witness of the Church to the world. Not that devastating criticism of other people, including their clothes, is unknown outside the Church and in society. Actually it is rife and women cannot escape the charge. Read your Balzac telling of Parisian cultural circles, so-called, in their nineteenth century, if you must know the worst. But there is another reason why criticism of people in the wrong sense must be dropped from church life. It is because the church is properly the refuge of sinners come for deliverance – it is not the show-case of the perfect. So read people but do not condemn them. I speak to myself as well. Criticism of others is a sin that 'doth so easily beset us' as the authorized version of Hebrews, chapter 12, expresses it. It is an encumbrance we must learn to throw off.

And now *fear*. The same letter to the Hebrews (2.15), talks about people who '*through fear of death were all their life-time subject to bondage*'. This is what fear does. It ties us up in knots. And fear of death is by no means the only fear. There is fear of tomorrow. Fear of a heart attack. Fear of cancer. Fear of losing all our money. Fear of a Marxist take-over. Fear of a rival in business. I could go on. So could you. All these fears act like a drag on our running performance in the race of life. It is as if Zola Budd were equipped with a pair of men's army boots in which to compete in the Olympics. But can fear be thrown off? It takes some doing. And is it right to label fear a sin? Is not fear an essential instinct implanted in human nature necessary for its survival? If we did not fear the storm we should not provide the shelter which saves us from drowning. Yes, but all sins are perversions of something good. Not long ago I attended a lecture in which the lecturer developed this theme with respect to every one of the seven deadly sins. I was quite convinced. So fear has a proper function in the lives of all of us, but if we allow it to tie our hands and our feet it is a terrible encumbrance, and we must throw it away. There is only one real antidote to fear and that is trust in God, a subject we shall come to in due course on another devotional occasion.

3 *Confession*

I have labelled this address, 'Confessing our sins'. So far I have said nothing about confession. What I have done is to concentrate on the recognition of our sins. And for this reason, that we shall not confess our sins if we do not recognize that we have any, or at any rate none worth bothering about very much, like that white lie we told last week or that stationery we lifted from the office a few days ago. What I am sure about, because I know myself, is this. We have sins in the form of encumbrances and we do well first of all on Ash Wednesday to admit their existence. Then we may confess them. To ourselves first and then to God. Possibly to some other wise and discreet counsellor, maybe a confessor. It is a psychological fact, quite apart from theology altogether, that confession relieves tension. I shall never forget how, at least thirty-five years ago, a non-churchgoing scientist who lived close to our vicarage, sought me out to tell me that twelve hours previously when he was enjoying himself, his son had placed his head on a railway line for the fast train out of Euston to do its worst, and it did. He felt himself responsible for the boy's misery. I have never seen a man more distraught. He writhed in an agony of guilt. He had to tell someone, and that someone was me, a complete stranger.

'Let us confess our sins in penitence and faith' says the priest so undramatically in the Eucharist Rite A of The Alternative Service Book. Perhaps it merely rolls over us. Perhaps over him too. If so, this devotional occasion on Ash Wednesday will not have been in vain if it puts content and solemnity into that phrase. It could make all the difference to our winning or failing to win the race of life every one of us is running.

2 Penitence

Luke 18.13 (NEB) *O God, have mercy on me, sinner that I am.*

'Let us confess our sins, in penitence and faith.' Thus the invitation to confess our sins in the Eucharist. We have heard the words many times. Let us be honest, we have heard them so many times, they make little impression. Penitence. What *is* penitence? What is repentance? What am I supposed to do as a worshipper on this occasion? How am I supposed to react to the formula? At this point I raise the questions with only one purpose in mind – to justify my action in selecting this subject for our devotional occasion today – penitence.

1 *Penitence is important*

My first inclination – and surely understandable – is to go straight for an exegesis of our Lord's inimitable parable of the prodigal son. Let there be no mistake, I do see in this story the essential ingredients of penitence making it a classic on the subject. Even so, I have to ask myself if I recognize myself at all in this picture. It sets before us a wilful young man brought so low by his reaction against what he supposes is the unbearable stuffiness of his parental home, that he romps through the whole of his financial inheritance and lands up in a pigsty – no fun for a Jew – with nothing better to eat than their swill. The man stinks and his dead eyes presage the deadness that will overtake him body and soul before long. When I lived south of the river in London I used to see half-a-dozen men sunk to these depths lounging on a bench near a shopping precinct, half drunk on cider even by eight o'clock in the morning. They were there every day. The same men. Always half dead though quite young. I used to wonder – were they prodigal sons?

It is the luridness of this story which prevents me from seeing a reflection of myself in it. So I turn to another parable Jesus told about penitence, also in St Luke's gospel (chapter 18). It is about two men who went up to the temple to pray. Here surely is a situation closer to mine and, dare I suggest? closer also to yours. After all here we are gathered in a place of prayer. We are not coming to our senses in a pigsty like the prodigal son.

I am not sure to which of these two men I approximate, the one up at the front or the one at the back. There was no penitence on the lips of the former let alone in his heart, but is there any in mine? Of course I repeat the words. So do you. But is there any penitence? Penitence for what? I am neither greedy, dishonest nor adulterous. I attend church. I give a proportion of my income to the church and to charities. I may not say so in church or preen my feathers like the man up at the front in our Lord's parable, but my list of sins from which I am free and my good points are much like his. So maybe I am a Pharisee too. Perhaps this is the thing of which I ought to repent, my tacit spiritual self-satisfaction.

And what about the other man, the one at the back. Fortunate for him, of course, that he could slip in unobtrusively. It was, by the way, a great pity when St Peter's church, Windmill Street, in London's West End, was knocked down and the site sold. It was tucked away in the heart of prostitute land. There were no marble steps to mount by way of entry, no forecourt to be seen. You could slip along this unpretentious narrow street and into this unpretentious church. There, where there was an understanding priest, you could confess your sins in penitence as not a few caught up in the prostitution racket did. The man at the back in our Lord's parable would have fitted into St Peter's, Windmill Street. There was nothing in his life for which he felt able to raise his eyes to heaven; no church-going, no subscriptions to good causes, with or without covenants. But there was penitence. He *beat upon his breast, saying, 'O God, have mercy on me, sinner that I am.'* On which Jesus made this forthright comment, *'It was this man, I tell you, and not the other, who went home acquitted of his sins.'*

So penitence is important not only for prodigal sons in pigsties but for Pharisees and publicans going up to the temple to pray. Penitence is important for church-goers, otherwise when the service is over and we go home we are not *justified* (as the Greek has it here), we are not reckoned in God's sight as good people, notwithstanding our church-going.

2 *Penitence for looking down on people*

But of what ought I to repent? of what ought you to repent? It could be Pharisaism. We must not fall into the trap of dubbing all those Pharisees of our Lord's day as downright hypocrites. Fussy they may have been over small points of the ritual law, but there are worse sins then getting 'worked up' over the way vestments are worn at the Eucharist or the infelicities in the wording of the new Alternative Service Book. The Pharisees did uphold decent standards of behaviour at a time when all that was best in the common life of the people seemed to be slipping away. We know the feeling. The trouble was they looked down on people. It was of that superior attitude they needed to repent. Otherwise, in the divine reckoning they were not good people.

Do we look down on people? Do we look down on those rowdies who line the terraces at football matches? I confess I find it difficult not to. Do we look down on those men and women who crowd the bingo halls and can rise to no higher level of thinking? Do we look down on militant trade unionists? Do we look down on directors who make big financial profits? Do we look down on those whose only school was the local comprehensive? Do we look down on old boys from Eton and Winchester? – 'My God, I thank thee I am not as the rest of men', coarse and low-brow. 'My God, I thank thee I am not as the rest of men', snobs and self-important.

Perhaps after all, I am in the company of the man at the front when I go up to the temple to pray when I ought to be at the back – 'O God, have mercy on me, sinner that I am.' I do look down on the irreligious and people who are not of my class, whether higher or lower. If the truth must be told in church before God, I am a bit of a Pharisee, and if I am not penitent God will not see me going down to my house justified, he will not account me a good man for all my undoubted devotion and charitable works.

3 *The composite nature of penitence*

But what is penitence? Is it *recognition* of my sins? Is it *feeling*? Is it a *determination to change* my attitude and my actions? It is all three.

It is not necessary to possess a profound knowledge of psychology to understand how our actions invariably involve thinking, feeling and willing. Not that they operate one after the other in an orderly sequence, they operate together in a comprehensive movement. We think and feel and act. So it is with penitence. We think, that is to say we recognize our

28

failings, we admit our sins. We know quite well what they are if we admit them at all – but this is not repentance. It is not penitence. The result may be defiance. The acts of violence on the picket lines during the miners' strike were not denied, they were excused, even justified. The 'scabs' *deserved* the rough handling. Nor is feeling alone equivalent to repentance. A man may feel sorry for what he has done, but his feelings may produce nothing more than misery about himself, in extreme cases leading to despair or remorse. If penitence can achieve no more than this then let us away with it. Nor is penitence simply willing, that is a determination to change the course of action. Such may devolve from prudence. 'I hate my employer, I count him "a rotter", but I intend to give up fiddling his wretched accounts because if I don't I may lose my job.' To be of value, repentance involves thinking *and* feeling *and* willing, all three. Perhaps this is set out nowhere more clearly, if a bit quaintly, than in the Shorter Catechism familiar to many Scotsmen. 'Repentance unto life is a saving grace, whereby a sinner, out of a true sense of his sin and apprehension of the mercy of God in Christ, doth with grief and hatred of his sin turn from it unto God, with full purpose of, and endeavour after new obedience.'

It is important to observe how the issue of penitence is a practical down-to-earth determination to amend our ways in future. This does not mean *doing penance* with the aim of outweighing our bad deeds by increasing the tally of our good deeds. It is impossible to run a credit balance with God. We cannot cancel out the past by piling good deeds on top of it in the future. But the past can be cancelled. It is dealt with by God's forgiveness guaranteed by Christ and in no other way. Otherwise we have no assurance. Our new life starts from God's mercy and only from there.

4 What brings us to penitence?

There is one other question to ask. What brings anyone to the point of penitence? Why should we want to repent of our sins? A simple answer may be the right answer – because we are miserable with ourselves. Nothing very lofty here, I grant; but

29

then the penitence of the prodigal son in our Lord's parable had no more lofty beginning than the misery of an empty stomach and nausea with sharing the pigs' swill. Not much in the way of spiritual aesthetics here. Yet his revulsion impelled his start in the right direction and it is the direction that counts, not the starting point.

For all the truth of this, and it is profoundly true, it will probably not fit our case on this devotional occasion. As I have already said – we are not in a pigsty and I guess we are not hungry and probably never have been. What is more likely to move people like ourselves in the direction of penitence is the recognition of goodness in someone we encounter, which shames us into feeling how far short we fall from their standard.

Not long ago, I read an account of the experience of a young Australian who served in Bomber Command in the RAF during the last war. I suppose his sensitive and vivid description of what it was really like to have to fly night after night into that inferno of anti-aircraft fire over Germany bit into me, because we lived on the east coast of England during the first three years of the war before we moved into central London. I remember the sinking feeling in the pit of my stomach as my wife and I stood watching night after night the seemingly endless trail of heavy aircraft droning out across the sea on their terrible mission, a very high percentage of which never came back. Each bomber crew had to fly thirty missions. Very few survived thirty, ten was more likely. For this young Australian there came an occasion when he was given two days' unexpected leave after a terrible incident over Denmark. Craving for peace and quiet away from it all, he found himself in the south of England at a village called Charlwood, near Horley. There he stood looking at the church, a grey stone building with a tower. The peace was unbelievable. A woman with a shopping basket appeared. It was all so homely. She asked if he would like to be introduced to the rector. He said he would. They followed a path across a smooth lawn to the rectory and he noticed the ducks on the pond. The rector and his wife were kindness itself. Stranger though he was, they invited him to a meal. Hearing what form his RAF service took, and knowing the terrible losses of Bomber Command and how young men had crossed the world to fight in the defence of Britain, they were apologetic about their peaceful surroundings. Then all three adjourned to the study. Suddenly the airman noticed the photographs of three young men on the mantelpiece. 'Are they your sons?' he enquired. 'Yes', came the reply, 'but they haven't been home for some time.' A silence ensued. Then the rector explained. Bob had been taken prisoner in Hong Kong and had escaped to Burma where he was fighting with Wingate. Pat, a major at twenty-two, had been taken prisoner at Singapore, and no news had come through for a year. Jim was in the North Africa campaign. . . . Another rather longer silence ensued. In it the Australian knew there were other kinds of anxiety and of courage besides flying Halifaxes and Lancaster bombers over the Ruhr.

When I finished reading this story the unostentatious courage of these people made me feel ashamed of the 'heavy weather' I have made sometimes over trials that fade into insignificance beside these. 'Let us confess our sins in penitence. . . .' It seems that God in his infinite mercy provides us from time to time with examples of a majesty of character that leads us to repent of *our painful mediocrity*. It is what the Lord Christ himself provides. When we see him we see what we ought to be and are not; but he is not only our humiliating example, he is also our saviour when on the other side of penitence we find our refuge in him.

3 Faith

Mark 9.24 (NEB) *'I have faith,' cried the boy's father; 'help me where faith falls short.'*

I wonder if you remember how on Ash Wednesday we concentrated our attention on the phrase 'confessing our sins' basing it on the invitation in the ASB Eucharist 'Let us confess our sins in penitence and faith'? Today, on this third devotional occasion in Lent I want to pass on to the word 'faith', 'Let us confess our sins . . . in *faith*'; and what I shall say today about faith is conditioned by what I said then about our sins.

Let me remind you. I did not deal with them as transgressions of laws of conduct. I might have done. Some sins are that, precisely that; murder, adultery and theft are examples. I doubt, however, if this interpretation is likely to fit our case. This is why the wording in the 1662 Communion Service seems overdone to most normal communicants – 'We are heartily sorry for these our misdoings; The remembrance of them is grievous unto us; The burden of them is intolerable.' And because this feels unrealistic for most of us most of the time we make no real confession at all when we repeat the words. So I followed the interpretation of sin covered by the Greek work *hamartia* – missing the mark. Our sins are our failures to live up to our own ideals. We are not the integrated and wholesome personalities we might be, and could be; and we know it. Our sins are the encumbrances that hinder us from achieving our best. It is over against these then, over against *hamartia*, missing the mark, that I am interpreting faith today.

1 *Faith in our Father's concern for our performance*

But where does faith fit into this interpretation of sin, or for that matter into any interpretation of sin? I fancy I can hear someone framing the question this way – 'I understand admitting sins, I understand being sorry for them, and the determination to do better next time – but why bring in faith?' This is the answer. Faith is brought in because of the frailty of our human nature. It is brought in because we cannot always do for ourselves, and with ourselves, what we would like to do. We need an external power to help us just as the sick man needs a doctor to help pull him out of the condition into which he has fallen.

Where do we look for this help? I believe other people are part of the answer. The instances are legion of young men and women inspired by the example of some outstanding person to

32

achieve a standard of attainment in their own life which otherwise would have been unlikely. To some extent all of us are drawn up in personal stature by copying others who unwittingly make their appeal, beginning possibly with our parents, then going on to our teachers. But these helps are not enough. They are not enough when breakdown occurs. They are not enough when we are sick with ourselves, certainly not when we cannot forgive ourselves for the blunders we have made. It is then, when we are alone and down, that we need the help of God.

Here, however, a large question arises. How do I know God cares, let alone will help? How do I know that the great architect of the universe has the slightest concern whether I sink or swim, whether I made a success of my life, or make a hopeless mess of it? Is it possible that God troubles about the circumstances that dog my performance in the race of life – my pride, my short temper, my laziness?

To accept that God does care calls for the exercise of faith. This is the faith that must accompany our penitence if it is to be effective. But is it so very unreasonable to exercise this faith? Let me put the matter this way. Here is a father whose son or daughter is about to sit O-levels, an important milestone in the race of his or her life. What sort of father would he be who couldn't care less whether they made the grade or not? Do not all decent parents actually live with their children's anxieties, hopes and setbacks at this time? I have had the experience of innocently enquiring of a couple how they were, only to receive the reply 'O, all right, but we have O-levels at the moment!' *We* have! They mean their children have.

If then God is our Father will he not be concerned how we make the grade in the continuous examination of life? Are we not his children, his adopted children? So is it unreasonable to exercise the faith that he cares what happens to us? and will hear when we turn to seek his help? This then is the faith that must accompany penitence, and what lies behind the invitation in the Eucharist – 'Let us confess our sins in penitence *and faith*', the faith that God cares about our performance, cares deeply.

33

And now another consideration. We believe God cares, but
has he the power to make something of us?

One of the most fascinating, I might almost say moving,
books I have read in recent years is called *The Agony and the
Ecstasy* by Irving Stone. It is about Michelangelo, the great
sculptor. When you stand looking at his Pietà, David or
Moses, it is hard to believe that they were once blocks of
marble. What consummate power there was in this man to
bring forth masterpieces such as these out of lumps of stone!
The figures almost seem to be alive. The minimum amount of
imagination is required to visualize them breaking into action.
They have expressions on their faces which even suggest that
they are thinking. And they all started as great blocks of rough
marble! It is hard to get over the wonder of it all. Only words
such as 'agony' and 'ecstasy' begin to cover the creative power
exercised in their making. But Michelangelo could do it *with
stone*.

What can God do with us who are common clay if we will
but open ourselves to his moulding? The way of opening is
faith, faith in his power to make us as he will. Not that we shall
all be made alike. Nor that we shall all be capable of cabinet
rank. But we shall be men and women able to run the race of
life well and complete it with a good end.

There is a striking picture in St Mark's gospel, chapter 9, of
the faith in God's power to make something far better out of us
than would otherwise be the case. It concerns an epileptic boy,
whose performance in life was ruined by his malady, causing
him at times to fall disastrously into the fire or into water. His
father, concerned of course as any decent father would be
about his plight, brought him to Jesus's disciples for the healing touch, but without result. They lacked the power to make
anything of this lump of humanity, if such an expression can
be pardoned of this wholly incapacitated boy. But Jesus made
something of him. He made something of him because his
father had faith that he could, faith sufficient anyway to bring
the boy. And the significant point in the story is that the
healing took place although the father's faith was thin, so thin

that Jesus rebuked him for its thinness. He had said, '*If it is at all possible for you, take pity on us and help us.*' At which we can guess Jesus turned his enquiring eyes on the man. '*If it is possible!*' he commented. '*Everything is possible to one who has faith.*' At which the reply was instantly forthcoming from the anxious father, '*I have faith, help me where my faith falls short.*' And the healing followed at once. The boy was made into a useful member of his family and community.

Is there any prayer that could be more appropriate for us in our penitence over our own shortcomings? 'I have faith. Help me where my faith falls short.' Help me to believe that you can make something out of me, something of stature. Lord, I confess my sins in penitence, but more than that, I confess them in *faith*, faith in your power to make me according to your perfect will.

3 *Faith in the worthwhileness of life's struggle*

But is the struggle worth the effort? Effort is always required to run in any kind of race. Marathon races are popular these days. Thousands of people taking part in them, and thousands more watching, do not need to be told that these races are not possible without effort. And the race of life from the cradle to the grave is no different in this respect. Effort is required not only to set up a business but to keep at it. Effort is required to keep a home going. Effort is required to cut down on smoking, to abjure drug taking altogether, to be moderate in eating and drinking, if efficiency and reliability are to be obtained in life. But are efficiency and reliability the sum total of what is desirable in life? What about justice, kindness, generosity and compassion? What about self-sacrifice? What about service of others? What about creative and artistic skill? What about spirituality? Do not these operate as the *crown* of life?

But is the effort required worthwhile? This is the question. A positive answer will not be long in forthcoming where our comforts and conveniences are concerned. I heard of a boy at one of our public schools who puzzled his teachers because when he arrived in the sixth form he did no work at all but was 'bone lazy', whereas in the lower forms he had studied furiously. And then he owned up. He had put forth all that effort in order to reach the sixth because there a number of 'perks' would be available to him.

Many people, perhaps the majority of us, are ready to make an effort to secure our comforts, but what about those attainments for which there is no obvious advantage such as compassion, humility, self sacrifice and service? Are they worth the effort? There is no obvious reward. Is it not far easier to go with the crowd and be governed mainly by the consideration, 'What can I get out of this'?

So my question. Is the moral struggle worth the effort? It is at this point that faith once again comes into its own. If I believe that the race of life leads somewhere; if I believe that we are not merely going round in circles with nothing beyond birth-death-rebirth-death but that there is a winning post, there is a goal at the end, I shall indeed count life's effort worthwhile. Life beyond the grave however – the goal at the end, cannot be proved though there are pointers. We can only believe it. It must remain for us a matter of faith. But *when* we believe in it the consequences are considerable, not least this, that the effort required to run the race of life well 'making a good end' is thoroughly worthwhile.

So faith in God's concern for us, faith in God's power to make something of us, faith in the worthwhileness of life's struggle is the climate in which we respond to the invitation in the Eucharist – 'Let us confess our sins in penitence and *faith*'. This faith is a form of personal trust. It is an attitude that lies on the other side of what may be called a kind of hunch that God and the eternal are realities, for this hunch may be little more than an intellectual attitude. No, the faith we are considering, the faith I hope we are expressing is *committal* to those beliefs, involving life now with the effort required. This is why 'we confess our sins in penitence and faith'. We do it because we trust in God, trust him with ourselves.

4 Keeping God's commandments

> 1 John 5.3 (RSV) *For this is the love of God that we keep his commandments. And his commandments are not burdensome.*

On these devotional occasions this Lent we have been thinking of life under the overall image of a race we are all called to run, the race of life. We thought of our sins under this figure, seeing them as encumbrances that hinder us from running well. It was of these that we repented. And faith, too, we saw as belief that God cared how we accomplish the race that is set before us, and also as belief that God possessed the power to make something of us as runners. Today, still with the invitation in the Eucharist before us – 'Let us confess our sins, in penitence and faith, firmly resolved to keep God's commandments' – we shall reflect on these commandments of God under the same image of running a race. We shall think of them as God's rules. God's instructions for accomplishing it well.

1 *Keeping God's commandments in order to succeed*

Some months ago it became necessary for me to purchase a new petrol driven lawn mower. It arrived from the dealer on a lorry and was deposited in my garden ready for use. Fortunately the salesman came with it and was only too willing to show me how to work the machine, for there was quite an array of controls to master. Nor was this all, he presented me with a handbook of instructions which he advised me to study. I did. There were two or three pages of rules. But I did not resent them. On the contrary, I welcomed them. I should have been lost without them. The mower would still be standing there, the grass uncut, and three feet high by September. And as if the handbook were not sufficient, in the autumn a set of instructions arrived from the manufacturers how to look after the machine in the winter. Rules and regulations! I did not resent even this last batch because I saw them as guidelines for efficient working.

There is no lack of people today uninstructed in the Christian faith whose unreflective reaction against religion is that it consists in essence of a boring assembly of rules of conduct, mainly negative, damping down if not robbing life altogether of its fun. I must confess I did not see my lawn mower's instructions that way. I suppose I might have done had I no intention of doing a decent job of keeping my lawns; but, given my wish to keep them, I instinctively knew I should derive more fun out of my new mower if it ran smoothly and well. So I received the book of rules willingly.

Now I admit there is a weakness in my analogy. We are considering the commandments of God, and God is not a lawn mower. Nor is he the manufacturer of lawn mowers. And when the latter sends me his book of rules he is not really concerned that I shall be happy in my garden, he is concerned to sell his product and obtain a good name for it in the lawn mower market. This then is why we cannot press too far the kind of analogy I have used. In our relations with God we are dealing not with a thing but with a person – or if we want to be accurate – with a God who is at least personal. And that person is concerned for us as a father is concerned for his children. He loves us and is concerned that we make a success of life, which may or may not mean a host of possessions. God's commandments are God's intimations for our welfare.

I am not sure if I have the right word here – intimations. God's commandments are God's intimations for our welfare, but I wanted something that carried the idea of fatherly advice or fatherly suggestion as to how we could best go about our lives, that is to say without any hint of a fiat, or threat or repressive measure subtly designed to preserve the gap between father and child. God's commandments are more like a father counselling his son – 'Son, I do wish you would get off to bed in reasonable time at nights, you are looking worn out and I fear a breakdown if you don't.'

No fiat here. No threat, but if you observe closely you will see there are consequences of disregarding the father's intimations – 'You are looking worn out and I fear a breakdown'. Note however the father does not inflict the breakdown as a punishment for disobedience. The punishment comes automatically as a consequence of disregarding the rules of efficient working, one of which is the need for sufficient sleep. This point needs to be made because judgement is a reality in the revelation of God as given in the Bible. If all the emphasis is on the love of God to the exclusion of the operation of judgement, we distort the revelation. God does not force us to obey him. We are free to go our own ways but if we do he will not cushion us from the consequences of what turns out to be foolishness. God then is no tyrant, but neither is he soft. To have a respect for a soft father is difficult, to worship such a God would be impossible.

I am aware that I am presenting a closely reasoned argument which not all may be able to follow but my purpose is to present the commandments of God not as rules to be instinctively resisted but rather to be welcomed as designed for our welfare. As the writer of 1 John 5.3 has it – *his commandments are not burdensome*.

2 *Keeping God's commandments to express love*

And now a step further. God's commandments, I have said, are for our welfare so that we may run the race of life well. What then is my motive for keeping them? Why do I obey? From what I have said so far the answer could be – because by doing so I shall be better off. This is true, but if this is all it leaves me in the centre of the picture. I resolve to keep God's commandments *for my own sake*. This is religious self-centredness and it is not attractive. Is there no better way?

Let me tell you a story. It is about a law student in Paris whose widowed mother and sister in the south of France scraped together all the money they could to make it possible for this one beloved and good-looking son to enter the university. They even cut down on their food and clothing in order to send him the cash, not only for his tuition fees but so that he could see something of Paris. But there were temptations in Paris especially for a young man with charm. And he fell for them in a big way. But what saved him from complete ruin was not fear of punishment nor even of reaping the inevitable reward of his moral transgressions, running into crippling and humiliating debt, it was the remembrance of his mother and sister back home and all the sacrifice they had made to make it possible for him to be in Paris at all. He knew they had done it out of sheer love. They had nothing to gain for themselves except the satisfaction of seeing him succeed. No wonder he could not tell them how he was living. The pain for them he knew would be unbearable. So it was their love that checked him, evoking a corresponding love from him.

I posed the question, Is there no better motive for resolving to keep God's commandments than that they will make a better life for us if we do? Yes, there is. It is to keep them as an expression of our love for God who first loved us. God's love is a sacrificial love of which the cross of Christ is the supreme expression. 'God so loved the world that he gave.' Brought down to the simplest terms beyond which I cannot simplify it any further, it means: if there is any decency in us at all, how can we not wish to please him who has done so much for us?

There is a verse in the Psalms which expresses this succinctly. (119.32 BCP) *I will run the way of thy commandments: when thou hast set my heart at liberty*. It sums up the setting which the ten commandments occupy in the Old Testament. Nothing by way of behaviour is commanded of the Hebrew people until the delivery from the slavery in Egypt has taken place through God's gracious action. It was not accomplished on account of the excellence of the people, they were anything but excellent; no, their freedom was accorded them as a gift of God's free love, God's unmerited favour, called in theological terms grace. When God had acted out of love for them, the keeping of his commandments was looked for as their response from gratitude. First God acts for us; only then are we expected to act according to his will.

Lent therefore is not properly observed unless, throughout, the eye is kept on the climax, which is the cross of Christ where God gave. Without this there is no proper incentive for keeping God's commandments, no proper incentive for confessing our sins, none for penitence and none for looking to God in faith. Unless our obedience is the outcome of corresponding love it will be self-centred, and this is not the way of salvation.

40

Come back to the invitation in the Eucharist. 'Let us confess
our sins, in penitence and faith, firmly resolved to keep God's
commandments.' What are they? They include the ten commandments, the decalogue. I mention them because we can be
trapped into thinking they do not really apply to the Christian
Church. We are spiritually superior to the sins they castigate,
I shouldn't wonder. Nevertheless they should be kept before
the Church. No doubt we know nothing of temptation to murder but what about hate? What about an adulterous eye?
What about stealing someone's good name? And false witness? Well, not in court; but what about telling half-truths
about people? And then covetousness or envy. Has it not
eaten into contemporary life in a widespread fashion? Are we
sure it has by-passed the Church? Are we sure it has by-
passed us?

No, we cannot afford to adopt a superior attitude to the
decalogue as if we were immune from the sins it covers. Our
Lord however summed up these commandments under two
heads which clearly impinge on us. We are to love God with
all our heart, soul, mind and strength, and our neighbour as
ourselves. I agree love cannot be ordered or commanded. It
either happens or it doesn't. Love is a form of response. We
can, however, be *reminded* of our love. We can be bidden to
show it rather more clearly. It is all very well for the husband
to insist that he loves his wife, but you would wonder if you
saw them together. And when did he last tell her that he loved
her? Love has to be shown if it is to survive, let alone grow.
This is why we are told to love God and love our neighbour.

But how? Certainly not by neglecting worship, prayer and
Bible study. Certainly not by treating people as cogs in the
community wheel instead of human beings with feelings.
There is a Christian life-style towards assistants in shops, gar-
ages and offices. If we interpret God's commandments in this
way, that is, as commandments to love, we should not write off
as irrelevant for people like ourselves this phrase from the
invitation to confess our sins in penitence and faith, *firmly
resolved to keep God's commandments*. Most of us have room for

41

rather more resolve and rather more success in this department of our lives.

Here then is this striking, if not startling conclusion. We shall run the race of life more successfully if, recognizing God's sacrificial love for us, we love him in return and our neighbour as ourselves. Perhaps we never thought of love as making for a good track record, but in the light of the New Testament this is how it is.

5 Living in love and peace

Some months ago I found my attention caught by a drawing of three little girls, sisters, the eldest not yet eight. It was designed to advertise a book called *The Suitcases*, by Ann Hall Whitt, published in the USA in 1982; and, sure enough, each little girl was either holding or standing beside a cheap cardboard suitcase. They were orphans but did not know what an orphan was till their mother died and their father deserted them. So a forbidding woman in black appeared to drive them away, where and why they had no idea. They found themselves in a religious home, stiff with rules and silence. Tearful and afraid, they clung to those suitcases, the only evidence of ever having belonged to anybody or anything. But it was not long before the woman in black reappeared in order to convey them first to a grim orphanage, and then to one uninviting foster home after another. Three drab little girls, in drab little brown dresses, the middle one with ugly steel-rimmed spectacles, each child, whom no one really wanted, struggling with a suitcase. Finally they were driven to the house of a young couple with a baby girl of their own in North Carolina to stay for one week while the woman in black searched for yet another home. When the week was up she did not return and the three girls were puzzled. She never did return. They could not believe it. This young couple really had received them with open hearts instead of the closed hearts and tight-lipped faces in every other home. And then it happened. It constituted their turning point in security. One day they saw their mother, as at last they dared to call her (to her great joy), actually burning up those cardboard suitcases on a bonfire in the garden. So they knew they were at journey's end, safe home at last. And from the warmth of their Christian home, where there was love and peace with all men, there developed in due time three fine responsible women, now married with children of their own, still alive and well today in the USA, for this is a true story.

There is such a thing as a Christian life-style; and it does not matter how fervently we may seem to have confessed our sins 'in penitence, firmly resolved to keep God's commandments', there can have been no reality in the exercise unless this life-style to some degree is evident in the form of 'living in love and peace with all men', or, if you must be up-to-date, 'with all men, women and children' yes, even be the children only three drab little girls with suitcases, committed to one's care. This life-style may be exemplified by one characteristic – *open-heartedness*. It should mark out every Christian.

Perhaps we might be forgiven for thinking at first that this formidable practice – confessing our sins 'in penitence and faith, firmly resolved to keep God's commandments' is bound to produce a sort of grim determination. And let us admit it, Church people do exist who in their moral faithfulness develop a certain repellent quality; they exude no warmth, no open-heartedness, no marked evidence of living in love and peace with all men, indeed they are quick to find fault.

Something has gone radically wrong here, and I mean radically, something has gone wrong at the roots of their basic reponse to God. These people are straining all their efforts to live up to what God requires, but this we can never do. We cannot reach God's holiness. It is utterly beyond us. But we can accept what is the heart of the Christian gospel that God in Christ has come where we are, in all our impotence and need, to save and sanctify us. This we gladly receive, and the gladness and the reception transform us. This is what makes for the Christian life-style, characterized by 'living in love and peace with all men', approaching people with open-heartedness because God has been open-hearted with us.

Some months ago Shirley Williams, of the Social Democratic Party, recounted an experience of hers as a young woman many years earlier. Her mother wished her to enter Somerville College, Oxford, for which she had won a scholarship – no mean effort. But she did not want to go to Somerville; she preferred the London School of Economics. Her mother, however, with no little difficulty, did at least prevail on her to attend the interview at Somerville. She was received by the Principal. 'I don't want your rotten scholarship', said the young interviewee, or words to that effect, possibly stronger; and she tore in half the letter which conveyed the news of the award. This violent reaction was enough to turn any Principal into furious rejection of the candidate. But not this Principal. She sat down on the floor cross-legged and invited the angry young woman to do the same beside her. Instead of berating her, she treated her with open-heartedness, drawing her out. So Shirley Williams (as she became) entered Somerville College, Oxford, and no more loyal student was there, won over by the life-style of the Principal whose laugh was frequently heard up and down the corridors of the college. No repelling remoteness there.

Jesus once told a story about the ground of our forgiveness of people in a kind of upside down way. It was about a servant who refused to forgive his fellow servant for the miserable little debt he owed him, but had him imprisoned till he should pay up. What he had inconveniently forgotten was how his master had released him from a huge debt when he pleaded for forgiveness just as his own petty debtor had done. It is as we remember God's open-heartedness to us that we behave with open-heartedness to others. This is the Christian life-style and this is where it is grounded.

2 *Imperturbability*

I have been speaking as if open-heartedness were the sum total of the Christian life-style. This is not so. There is also peace with life. What I mean by this is more readily seen by contrasting it with resentment against life, that is the life that has come our way, a widespread and common attitude among people of all ages and all walks of life. It is inclined to break out into rebellion.

This kind of peace is often met initially with rejection because it appears tame. The young feel this, and I appreciate their feeling. I too, heartily dislike tameness. I am not, however, advocating sitting down and letting events take their course. I do not admire the lazy, the unambitious and the 'drop-outs'. I look for energy, resource and enterprise. Nor do I hold any brief for those who let injustice 'get away with it'. There is a time to stand up, speak up and organize. The Christian life-style however is not hectic, hectoring and always in a frantic hurry. I take my model from Jesus of Nazareth. A full life? – Yes. A busy life? – Yes; more than once people wondered how he had time to eat. A steadfast life? Certainly; fear and danger were not allowed to block his purpose. But – and this must be noted – of ranting there was none. Of complaining there was none. Of lack of time for ordinary people, not a trace. Instead a firm belief, quite unshakeable, that he was in the heavenly Father's hands, and nothing had befallen him or would befall him which was outside his purpose of love for him.

We may call this Christian imperturbability. It is summed up nowhere more forcibly than in Luther's famous words *'Hier stehe ich, ich kann nicht anders'*, 'Here I stand, I can do no other'. Fearful of what the issue might be, he had dared to embark on the journey from Wittenberg to Worms in 1521 to appear before the Emperor and before the Empire itself. Many tried to dissuade him but he replied, 'And even if they made a fire which stretched from Wittenberg to Worms, and right up to heaven, because it is demanded of me, I would still appear in the name of the Lord.' The Emperor tried to force him to recant his protestant position, but he did not. 'Here I stand, I can do no other.' Christian imperturbability. Luther showed it and no one who has studied him could ever call him tame.

I sensed something of this imperturbability in Archbishop William Temple, for I met him more than once. And for many who may not have met him the picture of this solid man going steadily about his full life during the Second World War, not least when he was wearing his tin hat, was most reassuring.

So now I understand the words of Jesus. *Peace I leave with you, my peace I give unto you. Let not your hearts be troubled, but believe in God, believe also in me.*

Christian imperturbability. Accepting the talents be they many or few, placed in our hands, and using them energetically; but without fuss, without frantic haste, without foolishness, quietly believing that this is what God wants us to do.

46

Here is another constituent of the Christian life-style – imperturbability.

3 Realism

Come back again to this phrase, this injunction 'to live in love and peace with all men'. Is this possible? I mean, is it possible to approach *all men* in this fashion? I go further, is it even right to do so? Was it right to love and live in peace with Hitler in 1939? Some of the German people, if not quite all, were willing to do this. Were they right? We know the answer. Do we not then have to interpret this phrase with realism? It just is not possible to live in love and peace with *all* men. St Paul certainly understood this for he wrote in his letter to the Christians in Rome (12.18) *If possible, so far as it lies with you, live at peace with all men.* Clearly he did not believe it was possible, there were exceptions.

So opposition to some there must be. But this does not mean the end of all love for them. Look at the matter this way. Here is a mother-daughter relationship. The girl is mad keen (as we say) to marry a most unsuitable man. It is not simply that the mother does not like his accent or the loud shirts he wears; no, everyone except the girl sees him as hopeless, he is in fact a scoundrel. Is the mother right to oppose the girl's wishes? She will have to be careful *how* she opposes, or she will hasten the accomplishment of that which she least wants. But must she not oppose? Does she, however, cease to love her daughter because she opposes? Does she not in fact oppose the marriage (although she cannot stop it) *because* she loves her daughter so much she cannot bear to see her ruining her own happiness?

This is the point I wish to make. Loving people does not necessarily mean agreeing with them. It may be necessary, it may be right, it may even be considerate actively to oppose them. What, however, it absolutely precluded is hate. Christians are not to hate anyone. Hate, not opposition, is the contrary to love. It must form no part of the Christian life-style.

Take this observation over to God. God loves every one of his creatures, including you and me. He hates nothing, as the Book of Common Prayer says, that he has made. This does not however mean that he will never oppose us. We need to understand that or we shall fall into the trap of counting the love of God a sentimental feeling, which it is not. The word may sound harsh in our ears, but St Paul wrote in his Romans letter of the *wrath* of God being revealed as well as his love being revealed. Perhaps we might read the word 'wrath' as 'opposition' if it helps us to grasp how love does not always allow the object of its love to have its own way.

I come back to where I began. There is a Christian life-style. It is summed up in the phrase *to live in love and peace with all men*. It is not unrealistic. It is not sentimental. It is however open-hearted and it is imperturbable. This is what should come out of kneeling before God in penitence and faith – a practical disposition, the response of gratitude to God for all that he has given us. It is a life-style our neighbour cannot help seeing. It will be a powerful testimony to our faith.

6 Forgiveness

> Colossians 2.14 (NEB) *For he has forgiven us all our sins; he has cancelled the bond which pledged us to the decrees of the law. It stood against us, but he has set it aside, nailing it to the cross.*

All our thinking together on these devotional occasions this Lent has been preparatory, no more and no less. It has been preparatory because looking forward not to what we do, cannot do, or would like to do, but to what God does – he forgives. He forgives our sins. This is what is indicated in the formula which has become familiar to our ears:

> *Almighty God,*
> *who forgives all who truly repent,*
> *have mercy upon you,*
> *pardon and deliver you from all your sins,*
> *confirm and strengthen you in all goodness*
> *and keep you in life eternal;*
> *through Jesus Christ our Lord.*

48

This is the trouble. The words have become so familiar the whole idea of divine forgiveness fails to strike us any longer as remarkable. But it is remarkable. In one of the most well-known chapters of the Old Testament – Isaiah 55 – there are these words:

> *For my thoughts are not your thoughts,*
> *and your ways are not my ways . . .*
> *For as the heavens are higher than the earth;*
> *so are my ways higher than your ways,*
> *and my thoughts than your thoughts;*

This doesn't surprise us. We would expect God to be superior to us in all that he does and thinks. But look at the context of these words! See to what they are referring! They refer to divine forgiveness.

> *Let the wicked abandon their ways*
> *and evil men their thoughts:*
> *let them return to the Lord, who will have pity on them,*
> *return to our God, for he will* freely forgive.

This is the point at which God differs from us and we from God. He freely forgives. We do not. We even find it hard to forgive ourselves when we have kicked over the traces or been guilty of some mean and shabby trick. What is more, it takes a big man to forgive others. Little men go on bearing grudges for ever. They 'take it out' of the offender or even work out a deliberate policy of revenge. Big men, however, know that but for the grace of God they might be in the offender's shoes themselves. They at least have warts even if not thumping great sins hidden away; so it is wise to be humble, lest someone with justification turns round and points the finger of scorn. So big men forgive . . . sometimes.

But is this why God forgives? Does he forgive because he is bigger even than the big man? A moment's reflection will reveal the hollowness of this argument. God has no warts. God has no need to keep a low profile for fear lest someone unearth his own misdeeds. God has no misdeeds. He could not be God if this were so. No, there is no similarity between even a big man's forgiveness of his fellows and God's forgiveness of us. God's forgiveness is *sui generis*. It stands in a class by itself. This is why Isaiah was so categorical

> *For my thoughts are not your thoughts,*
> *and your ways are not my ways.*
> *This is the very word of the Lord.*

God's forgiveness is unique.

2 *God's forgiveness is not cheap*

And now this. God's forgiveness is not cheap. It is in fact conditional. It is dependent on repentance. God cannot act like an indulgent parent and laugh off wrong-doing with such a phrase as 'boys will be boys'. With God there is no general amnesty all round irrespective of whether or not the sinner owns up to his sin and admits responsibility. Excuses will not work.

We may not like this. There is indeed a kind of woolly idea generally current that God to be a God of love must be indulgent. And some people ignorant of the gospels reckon Jesus to have been a mild and lenient figure, ready to offer forgiveness at all times to all and sundry. This is not so. God's forgiveness is not cheap. It is not cheap because it comes in answer to our penitence, and penitence is costly, it is humbling, even painful when it implies admission of guilt. Where, however, there is penitence there is forgiveness to the uttermost, forgiveness without limit, forgiveness if we commit and confess the same sins over and over again.

But this is not all. It is not all because, if it were all, our penitence would be the efficient agent for ridding us of our sins. Forgiveness would in that case be a *human* work. We might even quantify it, so the less penitence, the less forgiveness; the more penitence, the more forgiveness. And if our conscience really plagued us we could pile the penitence on, we could go about in sack-cloth and ashes, we could divest ourselves of large donations to good causes; in which case it would not be surprising if we began to reckon that we were earning our forgiveness by our penitence, if not actually buying it. There is in fact a long history of such penitence.

No, forgiveness, though not cheap because conditioned by our penitence, is not cheap for another and bigger reason. It is not cheap because God in Christ paid the price for it. I know that if there are theologians present they will be alerted at this. They will know the dangers of interpreting the atonement in forensic terms as if satisfaction had to be paid to the moral law. I too, know the dangers. But I also know that in the New Testament the forgiveness of sins is ultimately bound up with the cross of our Lord Jesus Christ. Did he not say, the night before his crucifixion, as he passed round the cup of wine at the last supper, *This is my blood of the new covenant which is shed for you and for many for the forgiveness of sins*? And is it not in remembrance of him, and in communion with him, that we drink of that cup in every Eucharist for the forgiveness of sins? And was not the main thrust of the apostolic preaching a call to repentance and faith in the crucified and risen Christ for the forgiveness of sins?

This is neither the time nor the place to enter upon a discussion of the various theories of the atonement; but this can be stated as fundamental New Testament teaching, that Christ by his death and resurrection made available God's forgiveness of sins for every one of every race, whatever said, thought, done or written. The cost was Jesus's life. This was the price of it, paid in the coinage of Jesus's sacrificial body and blood in death. God's forgiveness is not cheap. God paid. This is why his forgiveness is unlike ours. This is why it is unique.

So now we may understand. We do not receive God's forgiveness *because* we repent. We receive it as a gift when we hold out the hand of repentance. No one pays for a gift. The price has been paid. But the recipient does make himself as worthy of the gift as he can. In penitence and faith he firmly resolves to keep God's commandments and to live in love and peace with all men.

3 *Access*

And what are the results of the Christian experience of forgiveness? We have already mentioned the resolution to keep

God's commandments and to live in love and peace with all men. There is something even more important. It can be summed up in the word *access*. Many people, especially in the business world are familiar with an *access card*. It facilitates contracts. It provides an *entrée* where desirable. It eases the granting of financial credit. The parallel with the spiritual experience of forgiveness of sins is not of course exact, it could not be so, but in one point there is a close similarity – the removal of barriers. Forgiveness removes barriers. It removes the barriers to communion between us and God, the barriers being on our side.

Perhaps we may catch a glimpse of how this works in ordinary everyday life. A relationship between two people, say husband and wife, may become intolerably strained because one has let down the other badly. Normal relations are no longer possible. The two have to meet of course, even live together, but there is no joy in the association, and indeed that is precisely what the relationship has become, a mere association, uncreative, un-life-giving, if not actually dead. But suppose confession of the wrong enters in. Suppose forgiveness is both offered and received. Will not the barriers be removed and a living fellowship surmount the deadness?

This removal of the barriers between ourselves and God by means of accepting the gift of divine forgiveness for wrongs known and unknown, wrongs done, thought and planned, making communion possible, is the prime outcome of forgiveness. We may call it reconciliation. It does not mean the immediate removal of the consequences of sins. A man who has taken to drink in a big way will still need treatment for the results of alcoholism. A girl given over to drugs will have to take trouble to restore her shattered nervous and physical health. But as a consequence of forgiveness the sinner is open to God the healer and the healing, because the barriers are down. Immediate healing there may not be, but the doors are open to healing sooner or later, though where capital punishment obtains of course this cannot be.

Here then in brief is the lesson. Forgiveness means access, access to God through Jesus Christ our Lord.

Access, joy, confidence, a renewal of energy, all these are the consequences of the Christian experience of forgiveness. Perhaps one other result ought to be singled out – a forgiving spirit, the forgiven sinner should become a forgiving Christian. Where this is not so the sternness of God may be expected. If this be doubted, then the sharp-pointed parable of the unforgiving servant told by Jesus as recorded in St Matthew's gospel should be read.

Once again it needs to be emphasized that a forgiving spirit does not mean laxity with someone failing to live up to his own ideals. What it does mean is a readiness to forgive and to go on forgiving where there is penitence, even though through feebleness or folly breakdown recurs and recurs.

So the forgiven sinner is never harsh. There is all the world of difference between being harsh on others and standing firm on the life-style the New Testament expects of Christians. And there is all the world of difference between making excuses for people because we know we aren't oil paintings ourselves and being ready to forgive because God has forgiven us. The Christian's forgiving spirit is based on the unique forgiveness of God paid for with the precious blood of Christ, not merely on the ground of a good policy of keeping a low profile. The Christian forgiving spirit stems from Good Friday up to which all our meditations this Lent inevitably and properly lead.

Let me end with a story. It is about President Abraham Lincoln during the American Civil War of 1861. A lad from a farm in Vermont called William Scott volunteered to do double guard duty for a sick comrade but fell asleep at his post and was caught. The inevitable ensued, he was sentenced to death. Abraham Lincoln hearing of this visited the boy in prison, heard from him of his home and looked at his mother's photograph. Laying his hands on the boy's shoulder he said, 'My boy, you are not going to be shot when you tell me you just could not keep awake. I am going to trust you and send you back to your regiment. But I have been put to a great deal of trouble on your account. Now what I want to know is this – how are you going to pay my bill?' William Scott fell silent. Then he said that if the bill were not more than five or six hundred dollars he thought with his pay, help from his parents, a mortgage on the farm and some assistance from his comrades he might pay. 'But my bill is a great deal more than five or six hundred dollars,' replied Lincoln. 'Neither your bounty, nor your parents, nor your friends, nor even the farm can meet my bill. There is only one man in the world can pay my bill, and that is William Scott. If from this day William Scott does his duty, so that, when he comes to die, he can look me in the face as he does now and can say, "I have kept my promise, I have done my duty as a soldier", then my debt will be paid. Will you make this promise and try to keep it?' William did promise and not very long afterwards he was desperately wounded and died; but not before he could send a message to the President that he had tried to be a good soldier and would have paid the debt in full had he lived. And he thanked the President for the chance he gave him to fall like a soldier in battle.

No, forgiveness is not cheap. Whoever said it was.

IN HOLY WEEK

1 Rough Times

As I travelled in the train this afternoon from Surrey where I live I could not help thinking of my early connection with this city (Norwich). My father was buried here in 1918, the year of the great influenza epidemic, and I can just remember the little gathering of mourners in black. He was not a native of this city, but my mother was. They were rough times then and to help my widowed mother with the expense of bringing up my brother and me, we were sent here as little boys to our grandparents for our school holidays. They were very kind but I only half liked it. It wasn't home.

1 *A rough week*

Holy Week is an annual reminder of a rough time at the centre of the Christian faith, a reminder of a rough week. Everything about it was rough. It began rough. It ended rough. For months, maybe two years, maybe three, hands had been stretched out to grasp Jesus and destroy him, only waiting for the convenient opportunity. It came in the week we began to commemorate this evening in the cathedral. Judas betrayed him. Peter denied all knowledge of him. Caiaphas condemned him, Pilate crucified him, and the whole mob of people turned rough against him. The soldiers in the yard at the back of the praetorium got rough with a leather lash laced with leaden spikes. And the roughness piled up to the torture of crucifixion, the spitting, the blood and the stench. Evil hands were stretched out to grasp and afflict Jesus in Holy Week. It was a rough week. That is putting it mildly. The ASB has got it right with its introductory sentence from Psalm 140 for today's eucharistic rite. *Deliver me, O Lord, from evil men, preserve me from wicked men.*

2 *Rough hands*

Some time ago, I cannot recall where or when, I saw a drawing of a baby and all around him on every side were hands stretched out to grasp him, not loving hands but rough hands, all eager to possess him for their own nefarious purposes. I doubt whether many of us would wish to take so gloomy a view of the prospect before each one of us entering upon life's journey, but there is something in it. Life is a rough business. You never know what will get hold of it and spoil it. Some from privileged homes have been caught by wasters and been reduced to poverty. Some from Christian homes overtaken by secularism and now are atheists. Some, perhaps very many, have simply been caught by the prevailing hedonism of our time and now are feeble unimpressive characters. So maybe there is some truth in the picture I remember. Rough hands are stretched out to grasp us almost as soon as we begin our lives. It is a rough world. Jesus knew it. It must be why he included that petition in the prayer he gave us, the Lord's prayer, *Lead us not into temptation, but deliver us from evil.*

(a) Blindness of heart

One of the forms of prayer appropriately used in Holy Week is the Litany. It pleads for deliverance, listing out the rough hands that seek to grip the souls even of the best of us, and taking up the refrain over and over again 'Good Lord, deliver us'.

There is the petition which runs *From all blindness of heart; from pride, vainglory, and hypocrisy; from envy, hatred, and malice, and all uncharitableness, Good Lord, deliver us.*

Here is a prayer for the successful man, the man who is somebody and knows he is somebody. He can't help knowing it. That is the trouble. He could be a prominent politician, a business tycoon, an academic as in one of C. P. Snow's novels, yes, even a successful ecclesiastic. Unless these people are protected, as sure as night follows day, rough hands will have them in their grip and they will be suffering from blindness of heart, vainglory, and hypocrisy. And then what happens? All around them will froth and bubble – envy, hatred, malice and all uncharitableness.

And you and I sit pretty in the face of this. 'This is not me' you say, 'I am a nobody'. Maybe, but none of us can be sure. I have seen little people more full of their own importance than big people; so have you. Blindness of heart is the trouble. We cannot see ourselves as we really are. Creatures with minds and souls of course, but actually completely dependent on God for existence moment by moment. Each one of us is in God's hands, but rough hands persistently probe to pull us away.

(b) Changes and chances

Another hostile and grasping hand can be included under the general title, *the changes and chances of this mortal life*. Most of us know what this means in experience. You didn't want that illness to come when it did, it just hit you. You didn't want the weather to break just when you were about to take your summer holidays – and goodness knows you needed a spell in the sunshine just then. You didn't want one of those terrible east winds that can blow here in March and bring down a tree right in front of your car with terrible consequences.

The progress of science and technological expertise has done wonders to soften some of the harsher aspects of our earthly existence – what a boon North Sea gas has been to keep us warm! – but people still get killed by lightning, are drowned at sea, and fire consumes dwelling houses, piling up personal tragedies. And if plague, pestilence, and famine have been eliminated from Europe, they haven't from Ethiopia and the Sudan. And as for battle, murder and sudden death, they are on the streets of the most sophisticated capitals. Have you ever been burgled? I have, more than once. And mugging? I doubt if even this beautiful city is entirely free.

But is it right to pray for protection from the roughness of the rough times in which we all live? *From lightning and tempest; from battle and murder, and from sudden death, Good Lord, deliver us?* But you can't stop people praying for this! I'll wager that even atheists suddenly caught in an emergency pray to the God they say they don't believe in! It is part of human nature so to pray, and has been since the world began. But there is more to it than this. Not only we ourselves but the whole world is in the hollow of God's hand. Only one man has entirely believed this, however, and lived out its truth, and that is Jesus of Nazareth. But because he did he was able to perform those

57

wonderful works in answer to prayer. Yes, it is right to pray for God's protecting hands against the changes and chances of this mortal life, for the whole earth is the Lord's and we are not its playthings.

(c) Rebellion

One more grasping hand – a cunning one able to be summed up in one word – 'rebellion'. It is easy for us to get caught by the notion that if we rebel we are bound to be free. Acquiring freedom is what rebellion is supposed to be about. But is it? All too often it is exchanging one form of bondage for another. No doubt the Russian people were freed in 1917 from the tyranny of the Tsars, and it was harsh, but has the rebellion really brought freedom?

Perhaps there are occasions when rebellions have to be. This could be substantiated but they should always be last resort undertakings. In this they are similar to surgical operations for a serious illness. This kind of operation is painful, dangerous and requires time for recovery. Civil war is a terrible operation, so is industrial war. The Litany knows this but it goes even deeper. It prays that we may be delivered from the rough hands called *the spirit of rebellion*, that has reached out for the soul of our people almost everywhere. We see it in industry, education, the professions, yes, even in religion. There is a widespread revolt against tradition and orthodoxy. Granted tradition can be deadening and orthodoxy cramping. Reform may be necessary, but anything like hardness of heart in implementing it, careless of the effect on ordinary believing people, and certainly anything like open contempt for God's word and commandment, is a roughness from which we need to pray earnestly 'Good Lord, deliver us.'

3 *Hands of blessing*

I go back to where I began, Holy Week is a rough week. But come to think of it, how extraordinary that it should be called Holy Week. Why not *unholy* week? All the unholiness in people's hearts crept out of their holes and burrows, their nooks and crannies, in Jerusalem, and marched brazenly down the streets to crucify Jesus. Why Holy Week? Because something

58

holy was going on there, something distinctive, something set apart, the like of which has never been seen before or since. God in Christ was taking the rough times upon himself in order to expiate them of their final power. He was letting the rough outstretched hands break his bones so that he might break their power and be seen risen after the resurrection, with the marks of the breaking still upon him.

This is why this rough week we begin to commemorate in the cathedral tonight is called Holy Week. Could we ever so name some of the rough weeks that have broken over our lives or may break over them in the days to come? Not unless, I think, we have caught some glimpse of the spiritual truth able to be distilled from the events of the historical Holy Week, namely, that God can and does bring good out of evil, and even rough hands can in the end prove to be the hands of the blessing of God himself.

2 Times of Crisis

1 *From crisis to crisis*

This would be an odd cathedral, a grossly eccentric cathedral, if it did not observe Holy Week, because the very fact that the week is called 'holy' marks it out as a special week for Christians. Nevertheless, if you stop to think, there is something strange about it. Holy Week is crisis week; the entire mission of Jesus reached its crisis in this week, which of course is why we observe it. We commemorate, no, we do more than commemorate, we *identify* ourselves with that week, we enter into it. One can scarcely be a Christian, certainly not an informed and committed Christian, without coming to terms with it.

We don't like crises. How many of us, with exasperation in our voices, complain as we encounter the news bulletins day by day that we seem to do nothing but lurch from crisis to crisis. If it isn't an industrial dispute, it is a financial one, or a political one. On and on we go from crisis to crisis. No wonder the sports programmes or the fashion pages in the newspapers are turned to for relief; but even there disputes arise.

Come to think of it then, when we turn to religion, especially our Christian religion, we might have reckoned to be free of all crises and sailed instead into the tranquil waters of quiet reflection, sweet reasonableness, and a steady unruffled progress in the paths of goodness. But no, we are brought head on into a crisis, the crisis of Holy Week from which there issues a crisis symbol, *the* symbol of our faith, a cross which in itself tells of an ugly, horrible thing.

The whole Bible is all of one piece in this respect. Of the story it has to tell you could legitimately say that it lurches from crisis to crisis even up to the last two chapters which tell of the city of God which is not yet. And no sooner do we begin to thumb the Bible's pages than we encounter a man and a woman ejected from a paradisial garden, a flood sinking all but a remnant of life, a rich and successful man turning his back on his home and kindred in search or a country he knows not what. Then grinding slavery in Egypt, then a desperate escape across water and wasteland. Still no peace. Instead, battle after battle, followed by a little respite and a little glory, but not for long. Close on its heels come defeat, deportation and exile. Relentlessly the story runs till it reaches Holy Week and there at the end of the road sticks up this awful thing, a cross with a man on it, the best man the world has ever seen.

Can't we get away from crises? The cry is real. But the answer is, No, not so long as we are alive in this world. It is shot through with crises. And because the Bible impinges on life in this world, it too is shot through with crises; it is even dominated by one huge crisis, Jesus Christ crucified.

2 *The essence of crisis*

What is a crisis? It is a turning point. Here is a man desperately ill in hospital, he is in the intensive care unit. And the nursing staff reach the point of having to inform the anxious relatives that his illness has come to a crisis. What do they mean? They mean that now he will either recover, 'turn the corner' as we say, or he will succumb to the illness. A crisis is like reaching a bifurcation on a roadway, there is a parting of the ways. One road goes this way, the other road goes that way. What is quite impossible is to be on both roads at the same time.

Here then is the sharp point of a crisis. We cannot alter the situation. We can only come to terms with it. A decision is called for. Shall it be this road, or shall it be that? The temptation is to dither, and the dithering may lead to crumpling up. So the crisis becomes the place of defeat. All of which means that a crisis is always a searching test of the people called to face it. How will they react? Of some men, some women, it is sometimes commented 'He/she is all right, but no good in a crisis'. The words may indicate no more than an inability to make up the mind, but they may mean 'going to pieces'.

In one of the most sensitive stories about the reactions of a child that I have ever read (which could only have been written by a woman), Lillian Beckwith, the authoress, in her book *A Shine of Rainbows* (1984) tells of a dour Scot who lost his wife. Her unexpected illness and sudden death was a terrible crisis for this monosyllabic but devoted husband. He could not speak of it. He could not even exist with the reminders of her about their crofter's cottage. One day he collected all the pretty tablecloths she so loved and her gaily coloured aprons and made a bonfire of them down by the seashore, finally tossing her spectacles into the flames. It was the last straw. Their adopted child found the charred frames and brought them back to the bereaved man. To assert that this man went under in his crisis would be wrong, but to say that he was a better man for the way he faced his crisis would be wrong as well. The truth is, he failed in his crisis.

What I am implying here is that it is possible to gain from a crisis. 'Great crises produce great men' wrote John F. Kennedy. Maybe, but only at great cost. And when the bottom seems to have fallen out of life as in a love bereavement there appears nothing on which to start to achieve greatness. Strong men and strong women manage it, and some not all that strong, but they achieve it through faith in the one whose crisis we remember this Holy Week.

So we return to that week, that historic crisis week. With its ugly cross standing there, it cries aloud that humanity – indeed the very humanity of man – is only rescued from itself by and through a crisis; whereas we are deluded enough to reckon that we can make ourselves safe, through the operation of our own sweet reasonableness. All that is required is enlightenment (*Aufklärung* in German), science, social security and education, and the world will be a wonderful place in which to live. Will it? Look around. Have not all these existed for a century or more, coupled in the Victorian era with a belief in the inevitability of progress? What do we see? Is it not the uprising of the dark forces of terrorism, fanaticism, and violent irresponsibility? Higher standards of living alone just do not make for higher living standards.

Holy Week comes back therefore year by year to remind us of how the world is, when viewed without blinkers or rose-coloured spectacles. It reminds us that the human condition is such that it took God in Christ the awe-fulness of the crucifixion crisis to begin to deal with it. And we don't like it. We don't like admitting that humanity is unable to save itself. We don't like having to step down, turn round and begin by accepting what God has done for our salvation. So the crisis of Holy Week initiates a crisis in our view of life.

In the year 1919, a Swiss Protestant theologian called Karl Barth (1886–1968) published an epoch making book which was really a commentary on St Paul's Epistle to the Romans (*der Römerbrief*). What it contained was a radical reappraisal of the current optimistic continental thinking that man could work out his own salvation. It came to be called a theology of crisis, and although various aspects of that theology have been severely criticized, and with good reason, no theological thinking of a serious nature ever since has been possible without reckoning with what Karl Barth wrote.

This is what Holy Week sets before us – a crisis, a place where roads divide, and where a decision has to be made. Can we save ourselves? or must we begin with God's salvation wrought on our behalf?

And some of you listening to me are growing weary. The very mention of theology, let alone German theology, seems to indicate that none of this is for you. But isn't it? Do we not have to face crises in our own lives? Here is a professional man arrived at the age of retirement. It is a time of crisis. Here is a woman faced with the probability that she will not marry. It is a crisis. Here is a fitter, only fifty, but declared redundant at his factory. Here is an athlete who, because of a sudden illness, learns that he will never run again. Here is a school boy who has missed his last chance to enter a university, his great hope. There are crises upon crises which loom up before countless people. Life is stacked out with crises right up to the last crisis of all when we pass through the last gate of this mortal life.

Has the crisis of Holy Week anything to say to us? It has. Notably this, that if we reckon we can face our crises in our own strength unafraid and undefeated, we are deluding ourselves. Are we really better than the disciples of Jesus? In the crisis of Holy Week they all ran away. Would we have done any better? Our Lord, however, did not run away, and the whole rationale of our communion with him this week is that we shall renew ourselves as partakers of his salvation of us and of his strength, so as to free our own crisis without running away, or breaking or going berserk. John Kennedy in a speech at Indianapolis said that the word 'crisis' written in Chinese consists of two characters, the one meaning danger and the other meaning opportunity. Crises give us the opportunity to put our hands into the hands of God and to rise to new heights of personal stature.

Rome was not built in a day even if its foundations were laid in a day. Your salvation and my salvation, your wholeness and my wholeness are not built in a day even if the foundations of it were laid in that day when we recognized and accepted that God in Christ died in the crisis of Holy Week for us. We go on being saved, we go on being made whole as we grasp the opportunity to react positively and not negatively to the crises of life as they appear. And it may be that crises are there in our lives because without them we would not have the possibility of that kind of reaction which is salutary.

Of course the word 'crisis' frightens us but let us take heart. God was there in the crisis of Holy Week. God will be there in our crises, whatever they are. God even works through crises for our eternal welfare. This is what the Gospel of Christ says.

PRAYER

> *Lord, you were there in the crisis of Calvary.*
> *Let me feel your presence in the crises of life*
> *lest I panic and run away.*

3 Times of regret

> Mark 14.72 (AV) *And when he thought thereon, he wept.*

1 *Regrets widespread*

I wonder what the regrets are in your life. And you look at me puzzled. What a way to put it; just as if the existence of regrets in everyone's consciousness must be taken for granted. But is it not so? Again you come back. 'Take me, for instance', you say, 'I've been contented in my job, happy in my marriage, I've never done anyone down. I'm not saying there have been no ups and downs. I am not claiming to be a paragon of virtue, but no, I have no regrets at the way things have turned out.'

I am glad to hear it. No regrets? None at all? Have you never said anything you wished you'd never said? Have you never treated anyone with a degree of harshness about which, looking back, you are sorry? Is there nothing about you you would like forgotten?

And what about opportunities? Have you no regrets that certain openings for advancement did not come your way, say, when you were young? Or that by a hair's breadth you missed

64

those that nearly materialized – the man, the woman in the queue of interviewees in front of you was appointed to the job you wanted. Perhaps you threw away what chances you had.

No regrets, you say. Not even about your average or mediocre health? Not even about the texture of your skin or the colour of your hair? No regrets about the members of your family? their marriages? their life-style? All I can say is, you are a strange creature if you are completely without regrets of one kind or another; or you are a shallow, insensitive person? Every man or woman who thinks has regrets of one kind or another.

Even Paul, the apostle, had regrets about the way he had persecuted Christians before he saw the light on the Damascus road. And Peter, the foundation apostle of the Church, had regrets about the way he denied Christ when he was up for trial before the high priest, fearful for his own skin. *And when he thought thereon, he wept.*

I confess I never hear St Mark's account of Peter's denials in Holy Week without being deeply moved. The structure of the story itself is striking. There is Peter standing before a fire, his faked disinterested features half lit by the flickering flames. A young girl is staring at him. Suddenly she spits out her contemptuous accusation – 'You, too, were with this fellow from Nazareth' – which he flatly denies. Badly shaken but unable to tear himself away from the trial of his Master, he retreats to the forecourt. The girl watches, her suspicions aroused. 'This is one of them' she says. The bystanders hear what she says. Peter hears it, more than he hears a cock crowing eerily in the distance. Then the bystanders move in with their accusation – 'You are one of them. You come from Galilee.' Thoroughly alarmed now, Peter piles on his denials with cursing and swearing. Then once again that distant cock crowing bringing back his Master's warning, *Before the cock crows twice you will deny me thrice.* Then the curtain falls with three dramatic words in Greek, the second of which no one knows how to translate but which the Authorized Version has sensitively rendered, *And when he thought thereon, he wept.* It is embarrassing to see a man cry, especially a tough weather-beaten fisherman accustomed to dangerous situations. But

65

this one did just that, he cried, so deep were his regrets at what he had done.

2 *Dealing with regrets*

How do you deal with regrets? A newspaper heading caught my attention last September. 'U-boat skipper's regret.' This is what I read. Forty-two years ago in the Southern Atlantic, Karl Friedrich Merken, captain of a German submarine, torpedoed the British ship *City of Cairo* with two hundred and ninety-eight people on board. In an epic journey in open boats to St Helena, two hundred miles away, two hundred survived. They did so because Captain Merken gave them the course to steer before turning his U-boat for home. He said he was miserable at what he had done. He had not expected it to be a passenger ship. For forty-two years the regrets hung in his mind, till somehow it was arranged last September that he should meet seventeen of those survivors on board HMS *Belfast* moored next to Tower Bridge in the Port of London. Now seventy-nine, the occasion gave him the opportunity to deal with those regrets. It was touching to see two of the seventeen survivors accepting his apologies and putting their arms around the old man's shoulders.

How do you deal with regrets? We do not all have the opportunity that came Captain Merken's way. Very few do. And much depends on the kind of event which occasioned the regrets – situations which overtake us willy-nilly, and actions I dismissed an organist once brilliant but now by reason of age and illness long past the job – but he couldn't see it. He never got over that dismissal. It broke his heart.

There are roughly two kinds of event that may occasion regrets – situations which overtake us willy-nilly, and actions for which we are directly responsible.

(a) Regrets over situations
Take the situations which overtake us willy-nilly. Such could be a serious facial disfigurement – a birth mark. I can think of one such case. Regret about this could turn into resentment souring the whole of life. In the case I have in mind it did not happen. Or a regret can lead to a general sense of inferiority in

66

a man throughout all his working life because his brother won a scholarship to the local grammar school and he did not. Or again, regrets over being brought up in humble circumstances can turn a man or woman into an aggressive figure generally disliked. The only way to deal with this sort of regret, the regrets over situations for which we are not responsible, is to accept that this happened in faith. There is no other way to triumph over them.

(b) Regrets for actions
Then there are the regrets over actions for which we are bound to accept responsibility. We did this. We said that. How do we deal with these? It is possible to try minimizing the action. Pride lies behind this approach. We will not believe that such intelligent people as we are acted so foolishly. Or we try to slough off the responsibility. The excuse is not uncommon, 'There was nothing else I could do under the circumstances.' Possibly not. Sometimes we have to take the lesser of two evil courses, both of which we regret. What does *not* work is to force ourselves to try to forget what was, what is, regrettable.

The story can now be told, in fact is being told in a book recently published called *The Captain's Return*, of the ill-fated largest airship ever built called the R101. She was completed in 1930. On October 5 of that year at 7.30 p.m. she was uncoupled from her mooring mast at Cardington in Bedfordshire on a supposed flight to India, her first. By 2.09 a.m. she was a burning mass of wreckage in a field at Beauvais in France with all but eight of the fifty-four on board dead. Two of the survivors subsequently died. The country was shocked. Flags flew at half mast all over London. A memorial service was held in St Paul's Cathedral attended by royalty and the Prime Minister. The irony of the situation is that the flight had been ordered against the advice of the airship's captain, the complaint of the construction engineers about insufficient test flights, and an adverse weather forecast. Amidst personal rivalries and jealousies *the flight had been forced through for political reasons*. What a mountain of regrets there must have been in the autumn of 1930. It is to be wondered how they were ever dealt with – if ever they were.

I return to the story of Peter's denials. *When he thought thereon, he wept*. Peter triumphed over his regrets. He must have done or he would never have become the leader he did turn out to be, confident and strong. How? How was it then that that shabby act of his in the high priest's palace, so little different from Judas's act of betrayal, did not bring him down for ever into the dust? The truth is simple but profound. He accepted his Lord's forgiveness for what he had done. Some people, perhaps many people, find it hard to receive, for receiving involves humility of heart, but Peter did it. That is why his regrets about what he had done did not defeat him.

Is this kind of experience only to be found in the Bible? Here is an up-to-date story. It is about a holiday maker in Germany. He came to a church in Allgäu where the verger described the paintings and the sculptures. Every time Jesus was mentioned his face so lit up the visitor could not refrain from asking his story. He told it. 'I was brought up a Christian', he said, 'but when the Third Reich came, wholeheartedly I supported it and became a convinced National Socialist. War broke out and I joined the SS, obeying every command without scruple. Then the Nazi rule broke. The war was lost and I found myself in a prison camp. When I was released I longed to become a Christian again but could not. No church services helped. I could not believe. Last of all I sought out the confessional and there I poured our my guilt. And then it happened. I received God's forgiveness through Jesus Christ for what I had done. That is why his name means everything to me.'

Fanciful? sentimental? pietistic? Of course the reality of the experience can be explained away if we so wish. But does not the truth lie here, that regrets are not removed till we are willing to put them into the hands of God who is willing to take them and forgive what caused them, through Jesus Christ the Saviour? There is a text in Micah 7.19 which it is fitting for the regretful to take to themselves, *Thou wilt cast all our sins into the depths of the sea*. How much better than poor Tess's case as depicted in Hardy's moving lines:

> It wears me out to think of it,
>> To think of it;
> I cannot bear my fate as writ,
>> I'd have my life unbe;
> Would turn my memory to a blot,
>> Make every relic of me rot,
> My doings be as they were not,
>> And gone all trace of me!
>>> (*Faber Book of 20th Century Verse*, 1967)

Poor Tess! Poor Hardy! How much better to receive God's forgiveness. Perhaps the confession and absolution is as important as any part in our religious praxis, not least for our psychological welfare. It is the way to stand on our feet again whatever the past, and to lift our heads high.

PRAYER

> *Grant, we beseech thee, merciful Lord, to thy*
> *faithful people pardon and peace, that they may*
> *be cleansed from all their sins, and serve thee*
> *with a quiet mind; through Jesus Christ our Lord.*
>> (*Collect for Trinity 21 BCP*)

4 A time for inaction

> John 13.5 (RSV) *Then he poured water into a*
> *basin, and began to wash the disciples' feet.*

1 *Upside down*

Some time ago I heard this story. A young clergyman had been invited by the then Archbishiop of York to stay one night at his palace at Bishopthorpe, just outside York. Before going to bed the Archbishop asked his guest if he would like early morning tea, to which the enthusiastic reply came, 'Yes, please', and in the assurance of which he retired and slept soundly. Next morning, still more than half asleep, he heard a tap on his bedroom door. 'Come in', he grunted, expecting a butler or a housekeeper. But no, there was the Archbishop himself, fully dressed in purple cassock complete with pectoral cross, cup and saucer in hand, having obviously made the early morning tea himself. The guest in bed felt distinctly awkward, the situation seemed upside down. He, a very ordinary clergyman, being waited on by the Archbishop!

Something like this happened with Jesus's disciples. They were reclining at supper when in the course of the meal Jesus, their host, rose from the table, divested himself of his outer garment, girded himself with a towel, poured water into a basin and began to wash the disciples feet. If anyone performed this service it would have been carried out by a servant, and a lower one at that, probably a slave. Needless to say the action made the disciples feel awkward. The situation seemed upside down. After all, did they not call him 'Master' and 'Lord'? If anything, it was they who ought to be washing *his* feet.

Not surprisingly one disciple protested and not surprisingly it was Peter, always ready to open his mouth. *You Lord, washing my feet?* So the New English Bible rendering. And when Jesus persisted he resisted with vehemence. *You shall never wash my feet.* All the same he gave way. He did so because Jesus said, *If I do not wash you, you are not in fellowship with me.* Peter could hardly wait after that. So Jesus proceeded with the basin, the water and the towel tied round his waist. The splash of water must have been audible in a silent room. James, John, Andrew. They were all washed. He came to Judas who did not protest. Jesus washed his feet too.

2 *Too proud to be served*

What do we make of this? What does it mean? It means a number of things at a number of levels. We will content ourselves with one. If we would be in fellowship with Christ we must let him do something *for us*. Maybe we do not like the situation to be this way round. It seems upside down. We would much prefer to do something *for him*. We would like to record what we have, in fact, already done. There was that

70

generous donation we made for the repairs needed for our local church. There was that splendid response to the recent appeal for famine relief. There were those unobtrusive chores but necessary pieces of service that were carried out behind the scenes for Christ's sake, and with the best will in the world and all without an eye on any kudos to be gained thereby. But in the first place, I repeat, in the first place none of it puts us in fellowship with Christ. First of all we have to let Christ do something *for us*.

Some of us are too proud to let anyone do *anything* for us, let alone Christ. That is a pity. I read somewhere how desperately poor the great Dr Johnson was when a student at Oxford at the age of nineteen. Pembroke was his college. His feet appeared through his shoes. When, however, he opened his room door one day and saw that someone had left him a new pair he threw them away in indignation. He was too proud to allow anyone to do anything for *him*. Maybe, had he been more humble he need not have left Oxford without a degree, compelled by poverty.

3 *The condition of fellowship*

What is the something which Christ did for us which we all have to accept before we can have fellowship with him? It was an act of astonishing condescension symbolized, if you like sacramentalized, by his feet washing. There are three aspects to note.

First, the lowliness of the task. Before the supper started there had been an unseemly scramble for places. Everyone wanted to be at the top table, even next to the host. Surprising? But I can recall sitting opposite someone at a banquet who complained bitterly at the low place she had been allocated; and I know the trouble seating plans occasion at public functions. How awkward then in the upper room in Jerusalem that Maundy Thursday when the host did not merely leave the top table and go and recline at the bottom table but so to speak crawled under it and washed the guests' feet! In labelling this an act of astonishing condescension, have I not made a superlative understatement?

71

Secondly, the original feet washing was not the refined symbolic action we have made of it in our cathedrals and churches. What I read in a sensitive book by Karen Armstrong is nearer the mark. Entering a convent at the age of sixteen in 1962, she was made one day as an act of penance to crawl under the dining room table and wash the feet of the older nuns. Yes they were dedicated enough women, beautiful no doubt in their character, but their feet at their age in hot thick woolly stockings could hardly be described as beautiful; which of course was why Karen as a penance was made to wash them.

Thirdly, do not miss the timing of Jesus's action. It was carried out only hours before he stepped down to the most repulsive place possible, the crucifixion site on Skull Hill, just outside Jerusalem.

This surely is the message. Unless we accept the lowliness to which Jesus stooped in the incarnation and the crucifixion as done *for us*, we do not belong to his fellowship. This is what the feet washing at the last supper, the first Holy Communion, is saying, and it is no use doing a St Peter, it is no use protesting!

4 *The true worshippers*

A consequence of what we have been considering may possibly be misunderstood but we ought to face it.

In our modern contemporary church worship there is an urge, almost a compulsion for everyone to do something in the service. We call it congregational participation, and churches even get assessed by how much of it there is or how little. In so far as this represents a reaction against the priest 'doing it all up there', perhaps half hidden by an ornamental screen, his back to the people, and if not in Latin then in an unintelligible monotone, it is commendable. The whole congregation, priest and people, should be worshipping together; *but* if it means no one can be a real worshipper unless he is doing something, the reaction has gone too far.

I read somewhere the other day of a vicar who had such an awful dream he was glad to wake up. He was presiding at the

Eucharist, but there was no one outside the altar rail at all. The only people present, and there was quite a crowd, were gathered round him all doing something – concelebrants, acolytes, servers, taperers, readers, intercessors, a crucifer, office-bearers, wand holders . . . not a single person seemed in his dream to be there in order simply to let the crucified and risen Christ do something for him or her. The Eucharist as they saw it was the time for them, not him to take over the action. But is that right? What does Eucharist mean? Is it not giving of thanks, giving of thanks that Christ stooped so low *for us*? We must be humble enough to accept it and for once be willing to sit still.

5 *The basis for thanksgiving*

I come back to this divine condescension as represented by Christ's washing of the disciples' feet. Apparently there is no place too lowly, too humble, too drab, into which Christ is not willing to enter. So no heart too bitter, no mind too resentful, no personality too torn by doubts, even unorthodoxies, no home too broken, no conscience too guilty to which God is not willing to come with his refreshing, remaking ministry. There is only one situation to which even God has no access, no key, no force to unlock and that is the proud self-sufficient heart which says in effect 'Leave me alone, I'm all right, Jack. I wish for nothing to be done for me. Good day. Thank you very much.'

So we leave this devotional occasion on Maundy Thursday with a picture rarely seen in our stained glass windows – Jesus with a kind of washing-up towel tied round 'his middle'. We leave the picture not protesting but saying *sotto voce*, 'Thank you, Lord for what you did for us at Calvary'. That 'thank you', not our activity, brings in our salvation.

GOOD FRIDAY

1 No weeping please

> Luke 23.26–28 (RSV) *And as they led him away, they seized one Simon of Cyrene, who was coming from the country, and laid on him the cross, to carry it behind Jesus. And there followed him a great multitude of the people, and of women who bewailed and lamented him. But Jesus turning to them said, 'Daughters of Jerusalem, do not weep for me, but weep for yourselves and for your children.'*

The arrest of Jesus is over. The trials before the high priest and Pilate, the governor, are over. The barbarous flogging in the yard at the back of Pilate's residence is over. We come now to the procession. We are accustomed to processions on ecclesiastical occasions. We almost take them for granted, not least on Good Friday when we organize processions of witness in our streets. This procession was slow, excessively slow. It almost came to a halt and would have done had not an unsuspecting Cyrenian called Simon been forced to help. Jesus leading the procession had broken down. He could carry his cross no longer, not after that flogging. So the procession had to reform. Jesus staggering at the head, next the press-ganged Cyrenian from the bystanders carrying the cross, next a crowd of people, including women, bewailing and lamenting.

1 *The contribution of women*

It is the women I would have you notice because Jesus noticed them and actually spoke to them. St Luke has preserved his words. It was so like St Luke to bring the women into his passion narrative and thereby to soften the harsh crucifixion account we read in St Mark with no relief at all. Trust St Luke, that compassionate man, to find something tender in the ugliest background if he possibly can. So he tells us of the tears on the *via dolorosa*. Not everyone's eyes were blazing their hatred. Some were weeping. There was a little humanity left in that spiteful throng. It lay in the hearts of the women who were there. Twice more St Luke mentions women in this same chapter of his narrative *And all his acquaintances and the women who had followed him from Galilee stood at a distance and saw these things* (23.49). *And the women who had come with him from Galilee followed, and saw the tomb, and how his body was laid.* (23.55).

The women brought tears to this crucifixion scene, but do not jump to the conclusion that all women shed tears at crucifixions. There was no lack of women at the guillotine in the French Revolution who did not shed their tears. In our own day some of the fiercest calls for the reintroduction of flogging come from women. The truth is, the tears of the women on the processional route to the crucifixion site that first Good Friday tell us something about Jesus. He had a place for women, so they had a place for him, a place of tender care.

The fact is Jesus accepted women in a way Judaism never did, in spite of the honour given to mothers. Judaism is demonstrably a religion for males first of all. Not surprisingly, it is men who are in evidence on the Sabbath in synagogue worship. But Jesus made women feel he had an equal concern for them. And so we see him in the gospel records, especially St Luke's, not only through men's eyes but through women's eyes, the widow of Nain's eyes, Mary Magdalene's eyes, the Syrophoenician mother's eyes, Martha's eyes, Mary her sister's eyes; and every time they saw him, they saw him act with gentleness and receptiveness towards them. Then there were the parables. The woman who lost her precious piece of silver, her seeking for it made to liken God's seeking for us. The woman pleading with the unjust judge, showing us all how to persist with praying. The young women who went as bridesmaids to the bridegroom's feast, warning us of how not to get excluded from God's gracious presence. Christ did not put women on a lower level. He included women among his friends – Mary and Martha, Susanna, and Chuza, the wife of Herod's steward. And as if these facts are insufficient, it was a woman to whom he first appeared as the risen Christ.

Women owe a great deal to Christ, even those emancipated western women who are least aware of it. Certainly the women

75

on the *via dolorosa* that first Good Friday sensed their debt as they watched Jesus limp along, with Simon of Cyrene following in the procession to the execution site on Skull Hill outside the city walls. They sensed what they were losing, what Jerusalem was losing, what Judaism was losing, and so they wept. Theirs were the only tears we know of, almost the sole signs of sorrow in all that sordid sadistic spectacle. Thank God for women. Thank God for the tenderness of women. They take the harshness off a cruel world.

2 *Beware of sentiment*

And now we turn to hear what Jesus said to these wailing and lamenting women whom he had spotted in the crowds. *Daughters of Jerusalem, do not weep for me.* No weeping please! It is so easy to let the passion narrative, and even Good Friday as a whole, act as a sponge soaking up our surplus pity. There is an element in human nature, more in some people than in others, that is attracted to the spectacle of suffering, not out of cruelty but out of sympathy. After all there is a tragic element in human existence. Vergil expressed it in the memorable words, *Rerum lacrimae sunt* – 'there are tears of things'. This is why there has always been a theatre for tragedy and why the *adagio* movements and the funeral marches in classical music find a deeply moved audience at concerts. They touch an answering chord in the human heart, not least the heart of women where longing and love, suffering and sentiment alternate as strong constituents, not to be despised, of common life. Their existence is the ground of the women's weeping on the *via dolorosa*. Jesus of Nazareth whom they saw as so good, so beautiful, so strong – it was so like life, as so many women have come to experience it, that he of all people should perish. *O dies atra*, what a black day.

We ought not to despise sentiment, but we need to be careful of it. It can end in nothing but itself. All too readily sentiment is ready to enjoy identifying with tragedy on the stage of human life, providing it does not stray across the footlights only to hold back when it comes to doing something practical for that unattractive but tragic figure in the house next door.

Calvary can be just such a sponge to soak up our surplus sentiment leaving nothing over to work in practice for the broken, the bereaved and the unwanted in our modern world. Religion as sheer sentiment is almost useless. Religion to be wholesome needs a strong element of reason in it as well as a strong urge to practical service for those less fortunate than ourselves.

3 Why no weeping?

Come back to the procession, the first Good Friday procession. See Jesus turn back to speak to the women whose tears we can be sure were streaming down their faces, *Daughters of Jerusalem, do not weep for me, but weep for yourselves and for your children.*

Why no weeping for him? Because he was not treading that road in order to provide a mirror in which all the sorrows of the world could be reflected, though people have not been wanting who see in Christ's passion no more than this. No, Jesus walked to his cross in order to achieve something, something that should evoke our gratitute, our faith and a deep longing to work for others' good. He was not, he is not, like a beautiful flower withered in the scorching sun of men's fierce hatred, over whom we shed our tears of sympathy. Rather he is like a mountaineer climbing Everest, or like an explorer trekking against odds to the Pole; and both mountaineer and explorer accomplishing their stupendous tasks. Christ was out to conquer, out to wrest power by the sheer force of determination and faith, out to overcome those grim factors in the human situation which drag us down, and to do it completely alone and almost wholly without a shred of human sympathy. – Ah, but there were the women on the *via dolorosa*! And he did not fail, he did not turn aside from the upward track. He ploughed on, come flogging, come fainting, come blood, come crucifying, pain and pitiless mockery. Christ did not break, he did not whine, he did not rebel against the harshness of his task; he kept going all the way till at last he shouted, yes, he did, according to the gospel records, he shouted out – *tetelestai*

– it is finished. 'I have done it.' You do not weep for a man like this. No weeping please, unless they be tears of gratitude.

But what means this second half of Jesus's utterance to the women on the *via dolorosa*, *Daughters of Jerusalem, do not weep for me, but weep for yourselves and for your children*. The address, 'Daughters of Jerusalem', provides the key. Jesus could not rub out from his mind's eye the terrible catastrophe that would before long overcome Jerusalem because of rebellion against Rome, a futile rebellion. He could not close his mind to what would happen to the inhabitants of Jerusalem and to the daughters of Jerusalem when Rome would settle down to break its back by seige and sacking. There would be no mercy then. Jesus in pursuit of his aim and of his ministry did not put plans before people as leaders so often do. He cared about the women, those sentimental women, those women who had not really grasped what his life and work was really all about, but still he cared for them.

So, as we see the procession drag along the narrow street which we have come to call the *via dolorosa*, the sorrowful way, and out through the city gate, let us put away pity for Jesus of Nazareth. It is not required. Pity for sorrowing mankind, yes, a fund of pity for them. Prisoners in Russian gaols and psychiatric hospitals, prisoners in Britain, men and women browbeaten in Afghanistan, hungry and emaciated people in Ethiopia and the Sudan, blacks in South Africa forcibly segregated from their families, children suffering from leukaemia, anguished parents – the list is endless. Pity for all, just as Jesus had pity on those trapped Jerusalem women, but not pity for Jesus. Admiration is what we need for him, admiration that blossoms into faith in what he accomplished at Calvary for the bettering of this life and the safeguarding of that which is to come. 'Daughters of Jerusalem, no weeping please, faith instead. For it is faith in Christ that ultimately saves.'

2 Onlookers

Luke 23.35 (NEB) *The people stood looking on.*

At last we have reached the crucifixion site. The procession
had been very slow. Doubtless there was much pushing and
shoving, much catcalling and booing. There usually is with a
crowd. There certainly is with a near-eastern crowd. Feelings
are not concealed. So, through the gate in the city wall and out
to that ugly little skull-shaped hill which everyone knew as
Golgotha, it wound its way. Golgotha bore the same relation
to Jerusalem as Tyburn did to London. It was the place where
the gibbet stood. If you liked the macabre, and most people
did (that is one of the sad facts about human nature) you
trooped out there on a public holiday. It was quite a show, a
theatre with free seats.

I am not overplaying this aspect of our Lord's crucifixion.
At chapter 23 verse 48 St Luke has this revealing sentence,
'The crowd who had assembled for *the spectacle* . . .'. The word
for 'spectacle' is *theorian* in the Greek. It is only used here in
the New Testament. But the other word, also translated 'spectacle' where it occurs in 1 Corinthians 4.9, is *theatron* which
anybody can see is the origin of our word theatre. St Luke
actually used it in Acts 19.29 to describe the theatre at
Ephesus.

This is the point I am making. The crucifixion of Jesus was
conducted as on a stage. The site itself was an elevated one. It
was small hill. The victims and the spectators were on show
there. The members of the crowd – and it was considerable –
took up their places where they could see, and perhaps hear (I
do not know). The rulers, St Luke tells us, jeered. They must
have occupied the stalls, so to speak. Way at the back, again
according to St Luke, who in the preface of his gospel tells us
that he has gone over the whole course of events in detail –
way at the back stood Jesus's friends and the women who had
accompanied him from Galilee. They 'watched it all'. The
Romans who organized these public crucifixions as a deterrent
against political revolt intended of course that they should

serve as a spectacle. Skull hill was 'made for the job'. Doubtless it was a kind of 'listed' site. Quite a crowd could line up
there to watch. Maybe the city wall could serve as a kind of
remote gallery. I do not know. But St Luke has written this
down in unmistakable plainness about the whole show – 'the
people stood looking on'.

1 *What they saw*

What did they see? They saw, I suppose, three stout stakes
stuck in the rocky soil already set out for the job. They saw
three men, the three victims, fastened and nailed each to a
crossbeam and hauled up with pulleys on to those stakes, the
weight of their bodies supported on a kind of spike (Latin,
cornu) or saddle. A mocking cheer, I shouldn't wonder, went
up as a kind of curtain raiser. They saw four soldiers settle
themselves down for their duty watch close to the crosses and
to keep the crowds back. They saw them set down their pot of
sour wine for refreshment when the sun beat down. They saw
them bring out a dice and toss for the clothes of the central
victim. The soldiers were pleased with their perks, especially
the one who netted whole Jesus's outer robe. Perhaps he
waved it to the crowd. Perhaps it did for his girl friend's
favours. I notice all four gospels tell of this tossing for Jesus's
clothes. It was for them a last straw of humiliating devilment.
Little else happened for a while but the people looking on saw
the charge written out and pinned on Jesus's cross, *Rex
Judaeorum*. They didn't like that. They saw it as Rome's blat-
ant insult to the Jewish people. 'This is what ought to happen
to any king you put up.' They hadn't put him up but they felt
insulted all the same.

Then they saw what they expected. They saw, and perhaps
heard, the bandits on either side of Jesus bawl out their bitter
hatred of their torturers. It was their last chance to have their
fling at the accursed Romans. No matter what filth they
spouted now. Nothing worse could befall them now. But there
was no bawling from the middle cross. My guess is the guard
kept looking up perplexed by the silence. This was new. Who
was this man? What had he done? And why were the bandits

on either side blasting him? Clearly he wasn't one of them and they angrily resented his silence, till one at least seemed to be quietened by what the central victim whispered.

The time dragged. This was the trouble with these crucifixions, they dragged, even for days. More gruesome still it became so dark, according to the gospel accounts. The duty watch could scarcely see their victims, let alone the crowds standing still in serried ranks or sitting down to pass the time.

Just before three o'clock there was a bit of a stir and the clouds were lifting. They saw one of the guards move. Those close at hand heard what they least expected, a shout from the so-called 'king of the Jews'. All apparently was over. There was nothing else to see, except the soldiers finishing off the bandits with blows from a heavy mallet. This show had ended early.

2 *How they reacted*

If you are anything like me, and I expect you are, it is the callousness as well as the cruelty of all this which is so hateful. But it is no more callous and no more cruel than a terrorist today who can plant a bomb, operate the remote control, and watch from a safe distance the unsuspecting victim blown to pieces, knowing that friends and relatives will break down in bitter weeping, their lives now in little broken pieces. There was the Harrod's bomb, the Brighton bomb, the bomb planted on a train in Italy and exploded in a tunnel; and who knows how many bombs and booby traps in Northern Ireland? It is the callousness that brings us sometimes to the point of despair about human nature.

But I want to draw your attention to something else about this watching crowd in the theatre at Golgotha that first Good Friday, callous though it was at first. It became painfully uncomfortable. And could you have seen the people drifting back into the city, the show over, you would have seen none of the holiday mood with which they set out. There was no shouting, no catcalling. Instead a strange silence. More strange still, a number of people were actually beating their breasts. They sensed something had gone sorely wrong some-

81

where. That show on Skull Hill ought never to have been staged. The Romans, 'the blighters', had picked the wrong man. Wasn't there a robber called Barabbas all fixed for this? Where had he got to?

I don't know what to call this change of mood. Was it mere shock? Was it remorse? Was it repentance? or did the people simply feel shabby staring at a kind of saint in his final agony? We are all tempted to write off this breast-beating as nothing much, those of us who have seen enough of crowds to know their fickleness. But I wonder. I wonder if we ought to write it off so easily. Does not St Luke tell us in the book of the Acts of the Apostles that when, in a matter of only weeks, Peter and the other apostles began to proclaim Jesus as the Christ in this same city, there was a considerable turning in repentance and faith to this same Jesus?

Let us be careful how we write off these people as *hopelessly* shallow and fickle. Shallow and fickle may be, but hopelessly so? Jesus never wrote off people. We read he had compassion on the multitudes. They were never *la canaille* for him, they were sheep without a shepherd. Did they sense (I don't know, but I ask) did they sense standing there in their serried ranks that Good Friday in the theatre at Golgotha, just looking on, did they sense that he never hated *them*? They were used to being hated. The Romans hated the Jews' guts. Their own rulers, yes, even the priests, despised them as the unlettered mob, but Jesus loved them. Did they sense this? All we know for sure is, they went home beating their breasts. They'd seen the wrong man killed.

3 Looking and living

I don't like what I have set out in this sermon. I mean, there is that in me which would prefer as the centre point of my faith some sort of philosophy or some sort of ascetic discipline, better still, some sort of stupendous splendour to lift me out of my earthiness into aesthetic sensitivity, not a man on a gibbet and a crowd standing by to stare. But that is what the Christian gospel placards before us perpetuated in a thousand thousand churches in the form of a crucifix fixed upon the wall or standing on the altar.

82

There is a story in the Old Testament which tells of the children of Israel mortally bitten by serpents in the course of their desert trek to the land of Canaan. It tells of how Moses made a brazen image of one of those serpents and set it upon a pole for all to see. And those who did trouble to see and did not count the effort foolish, were cured of their complaint. A strange story. We do not know what to make of it.

But the writer of the fourth gospel knew what to make of it. Thinking of the crucifixion of Jesus in the theatre of Golgotha, this is what he wrote. 'As Moses lifted up the serpent in the wilderness, even so must the Son of Man be lifted up that whosoever believeth in him should not perish but have eternal life.'

There is something devastatingly simple about our Christian religion. All we have to do to receive eternal life which not even death will snatch away, is to look at the crucified Jesus without rejecting him. (See how low I have geared this.) I think the crowds that first Good Friday came to the point of seeing Jesus without rejecting him as they 'stood looking on'.

Perhaps that is all a Good Friday sermon like this can hope for, that we at least look at him who was crucified without rejecting him, that we all look and live, look and live eternally.

This anyway is the gospel of Christ.

3 Thirsting and longing

> John 19.28, 29 (NEB) *After that, Jesus, aware that all had now come to its appointed end, said in fulfilment of Scripture, 'I thirst'. A jar stood there full of sour wine; so they soaked a sponge with the wine, fixed it on a javelin, and held it up to his lips.*

The crucifixion scene has almost come to its end and we are about to see the curtain fall. Thank God for that! The cross was the most wicked thing ever invented. It came from the Phoenicians but the Romans took it over. We hate it. For its stark naked cruelty we are right to hate it. We must hate it before we begin to glorify it. At the humanitarian level as opposed to the theological, we must always hate it.

But we are also right not to rub out the cross on which Christ was crucified. We must not even draw a veil over it. Not least for this reason, that if we did, when we attempted to offer the Christian gospel to men and women at the end of their tether – and God knows, there are enough of them in the world when you think of the prison camps, the refugees and the starving thousands in Africa, let alone people known to be threatened with death from some incurable ailment – if we did suppress the ugly part of Jesus's end, every one of them could round on us and bitterly cry – 'What does your Christ know about my ghastly situation?'

No, I am not going to try and make out a case for Christ's sufferings being worse than any that have ever been endured. I have read, as you must have read, of tortures that have lasted longer than the hours of his crucifixion. In the far east as a punishment they'd sit a man just above a sprouting bamboo shoot till it grew up inside his bowels. It takes more than three hours. All I want to say is this. Jesus went down to the hell where hellish things like this are done. No, don't bring out the drapes to hide up those horrible hours of Jesus's end. You'll have no message for those whose feet have gone right through the floor boards at the bottom of life, down into the sewer, if you do. Jesus went where they are to rescue them. He descended into hell.

1 *Thirsting*

You see what I am doing. I am taking these words of Christ on the Cross, 'I thirst', first of all at their face value. His mouth was dry. His tongue was swollen. He was all but choking to death with the constriction of his throat and gullet. And when pain progresses to the point of blinding intensity, it is impossible to squeeze beyond it. It boxes the victim up inside it.

W. H. Auden has these four lines in his poem 'Surgical Ward':

> *'They come and suffer; that is all they do.*
> *A bandage hides the place where each is living.*
> *His knowledge of the world is restricted to*
> *the treatment that the instruments are giving.'*

What I am saying is this. Christ went down into the cage where life *equals* pain, that was all that was left of life for him then. I would like all who have ever known, or have ever not known, what pain does, to hear what I am saying.

'I thirst.' This is what the fourth gospel tells us Jesus said shortly before his end came. He called out from his cage of pain. A cry of pain is primarily what it was, the only one such cry in the records of the crucifixion. But I want to expand it a little. I want to remind you that he was dying as a man at work. It was work he was finishing on the cross. We shall consider this aspect in a moment in connection with the final words, *It is finished*. His work was our human redemption. What a work! What a colossal work! When you work hard, when you labour at lifting heavy loads, when you go on and on at the task, you become thirsty. Is it fanciful to hear in Jesus's cry, 'I thirst', the cry of a workman being worked to death for the superhuman task of reconciling us to God? See a man operating one of those pneumatic drills on the road. See his arms quivering, every muscle taut. Then he climbs out of the hole dug, his work finished. Watch him. He sits down by the roadside and reaches for a drink.

When Christ had all but finished his work on the cross he said, *I thirst*.

2 *The unknowing warrior*

Come back to the crucifixion site. Watch closely. In the half light there is a man approaching a stone jar set down close by the cross. It contained sour wine, the common soldiers' drink on duty. Soaking a sponge in the vinegary liquor this man stuck it on a javelin point (if this is how we are to read the Greek of the narrative here), and held it to his lips, because he had heard those faint words of half request, *I thirst*.

I have read these accounts, I shouldn't wonder, as carefully

85

as any in this congregation, and I guess that when this man, this soldier, went forward with that drink-soaked sponge other soldiers called out in caustic sarcasm, 'Cut it out man, let him be, he's calling old Elijah. See if he comes. Perhaps he'll cut him down.' And the soldier with the sponge joined in the ribaldry. He didn't fancy being called a softie. But he went forward with the sponge on the javelin point all the same. He gave Jesus to drink.

We do not know the name of this soldier. He was the unknowing warrior, but I can't help wondering, and maybe you can't help wondering, if years later, perhaps away in sunny Rome, back home with his wife and children, his military service over, he came across St Matthew's gospel, and this is what he read:

> When the Son of man shall come in his glory, and all the holy angels with him, then shall he sit upon the throne of his glory: And before him shall be gathered all nations: and he shall separate them one from another, as a shepherd separateth his sheep from the goats: ... Then shall the King say unto them on his right hand, Come, ye blessed of my Father, inherit the kingdom prepared for you from the foundation of the world: ... I was thirsty, and ye gave me drink.

Did he know what he was doing? I mean that Roman soldier that first Good Friday with the wine-soaked sponge on a javelin point? No, but out of his heart, not quite turned to stone by the cruelties he had to inflict, like some of those SS guards in the prisoner of war camps during the last war in Germany, there came a tiny spark of human kindness. I ask you, 'Do you think Jesus failed to notice? Do you think God failed to notice?' If you are in doubt read the parable of the sheep and the goats in Matthew Chapter 25, and you will recognize the rewards to be given for acts of common kindness even when carried out with no idea why they were done at all.

I ask. Is it possible for the generosity of God to go any further? Is it not on a par with what Jesus once said himself that whoever gives even a cup of cold water in the name of a disciple of Christ, he shall in no wise lose his reward?

The point I am making is this. The redemption worked out

by Christ on the cross reaches out to extremities beyond which there are no more extremities. The soldier with the drink-soaked sponge, the woman with a cup of cold water – well, you complete the list if you can, they are all included because somehow, however unknowingly, Christ was involved in what they did. He is their redeemer *even when they do not know it*.

We could of course proceed on the strength of this incident to encourage our acts of common human kindness, reliefs and charities, and that would be right, a thousand times right; but first of all, at the foot of the Cross on Skull Hill outside Jerusalem, let us see what work Christ did for the recovery of our humanity and the welfare of our souls.

3 *Longing*

We are near the end now. I do not know, and I cannot prove it, but I guess that throughout that horrifying crucifixion nightmare, as long as he was able to concentrate at all, Jesus prayed the Psalms which he knew by heart from a child. And in passing let me say this, that herein lies the value of remembered prayers whether from the Bible, the psalter or the hymn book, when some crisis overtakes us, say some debilitating illness or numbing bereavement, when to formulate any new thoughts is utterly impossible, then we have some appropriate words ready, and *they comfort*.

I suggest that on the cross Jesus recited Psalm 42.

> *Like as the hart desireth the waterbrooks:*
> *so longeth my soul after thee, O God.*
> *My soul is athirst for God, yea, even for the living God:*
> *when shall I come to appear before the presence of God?*

It could not, in the nature of the case, be long now. His strength was ebbing fast away. His head would soon fall and he would pass into the eternal presence. He had come to the time when he longed for the passing. *I thirst. My soul is athirst for God, when shall I come to appear before the presence of God?*

All his days Jesus had lived close to the unseen presence of God to an extent none of us ever achieve, but it was an unseen presence. That situation would soon end and he longed for it.

Is it ever wrong to want to die? Surely not when life has so closed in there is almost nothing left. I have witnessed this with the chronically sick and with those who (as we say) have outlived their span of years, for I have, in my time, been a parish priest. And as the years go by, the ranks of those we know and love become heartrendingly thin. It is understandable how real is the longing to depart and be with those who have gone on before.

> *And with the morn those angel faces smile,*
> *Which I have loved long since, and lost awhile.*

But is it ever anything else but morbid, if not actually to long for heaven, then to look expectantly towards it? I do not think it is morbid. I remember once hearing that ultra-extrovert Archbishop Fisher say he was looking forward to it because there were so many things he would like to know.

> *For now we see through a glass, darkly;*
> *but then face to face:*

or as the New English Bible puts it at 1 Corinthians 13.12, *Now we see only puzzling reflections in a mirror, but then we shall see face to face. My knowledge now is partial; then it will be whole, like God's knowledge of me.*

St Paul, in fact, said he was torn two ways. What he would like was to depart, and be with Christ; which is better by far, but for his work's sake there was greater need that he should stay in the body (Philippians 1.23).

I wonder if I could at least say this, that he/she is a poor Christian who is not sensitive to the promised blessings of heaven compared with the endless turmoils and sorrows of this world.

So we come almost to the time for the curtain to fall. The darkness began to lift before the end, making the three crosses more starkly prominent on that ugly hill where they were set. We cannot let this scene slip out of our Christian faith. This crucifixion happened. And because the man on the middle cross was so different, while yet being a man of flesh and blood like ourselves whom a cross could torture and kill, we have to

88

pay attention. The destiny of us all is wrapped up in what happened there. What happened is as crucial as that.

DURING EASTERTIDE

1 Union with the risen Christ

> Acts 2.24 (NEB) *But God raised him to life again, setting him free from the pangs of death, because it would not be that death should keep him in its grip.*

I wish I could have heard these words spoken instead of having to read them. I know this is a stupid wish, not least because they were probably spoken in Aramaic and I cannot understand Aramaic, but I would like to have heard where the accent was placed. Meaning is conveyed by a speaker through what he accentuates. As it happens I am convinced that the accent actually fell on the pronoun 'him' in this sentence '. . . because it could not be that death should keep *him* in its grip.'

You see, Easter is not about the resurrection of *anybody*. God did not raise up from the grave one of those eighteen on whom the tower at Siloam fell, nor one of those Galileans who were dutifully offering their sacrifices in the temple when Pilate cut them down. Easter Day is not simply a demonstration of what God can do, he can bring back a dead person to life. No doubt he can. And if we are not content to leave this in propositional form we may look into the gospels and read three accounts of him doing it – the restoration to life of the widow of Nain's son, Jairus's daughter and Lazarus of Bethany. But there is no gospel for me in what God is able to do. How do I know he will do it for me? How do I know he will do it for you?

No, Easter is not simply an exhibition of God's power, the meaning is much deeper, much more sweeping. It is to be sought in what the New Testament tells us; that it was *Jesus* whom God raised up. This is why I am quite sure that the accent falls on the personal pronoun in my text, 'But God raised him to life again . . . because it could not be that death should keep *him* in its grip.' Why not? I will give three reasons, and the first is that Jesus had to be justified.

Just think about Jesus of Nazareth. He was the nation's rejected man. At the end he was no one's hero. Hero was not a title even the handful of disciples in hiding on Good Friday, or the pitiful little knot of women watching the cruel dying of the man they loved, would have ever thought of employing. If for anyone at the crucifixion site the word might have been used, it would have been for the freedom fighters, the Zealots, the two bandits crucified with Jesus. They were at least raising a fist against the government. But Jesus? No. No one sang his praises at the end. They did earlier on in his ministry, they sang his praises on account of his wonderful works; but when he refused to be made their political king, a king who would overturn the status quo, with force if need be, they turned against him. Even so it was not this political pacifism which caused his rejection but his religious teaching. It was anathema to the hierarchy. He seemed to be standing the moral law on its head. He actually told the religious authorities to their faces that sinners would enter into the kingdom of God before them. And as if to demonstrate this teaching he 'hob-nobbed' with the riff-raff of the town for whom he appeared to cherish a special liking. You obviously accept those with whom you choose to mix. Clearly then Jesus accepted sinners. He offered them forgiveness. Their goodness or lack of goodness was not the condition of his friendship with them, but their willingness to count themselves as on his side – yes, as simple as that. All this was odious to the religious leaders of Jesus's day, and not only of his day. Therefore they rejected him. And the last they saw of him was as a dead man flanked in death on either side by two notorious sinners. 'Very well, that is what he wanted, now he has it'. Is this what they said? If so, the strange fact is, they were right.

Now suppose, just suppose, God had not raised Jesus from the dead. Suppose he had been left a reject in people's minds. Suppose he had appeared to no one after the crucifixion, not even to the closest of his followers – what would have become of his teaching? It would have been rejected as he was rejected. Here and there, maybe, for a few years, a handful of persons might wistfully have confessed as did Cleopas and his friend in Luke's moving story in Chapter 24 of his gospel – 'We had been hoping' – but not now. That extraordinary man Jesus, who seemed to be as close to God as it is possible to imagine, speaking as none other spoke the very words of God, God himself forsook. He did not reverse the nation's verdict that Jesus was a blasphemer. He did not justify the way he lived or the way he spoke. He simply let them go the way of all flesh.

The point I am making is this. Jesus had to be raised from the dead – 'it could not be that death should keep *him* in its grip' – if both he and his extraordinary teaching were to be justified. So the resurrection shows that Jesus was right after all. God does forgive repentant sinners. God does welcome them into his fellowship. This really is the Christian gospel. It is what the apostles stood up to preach immediately after the resurrection. They would not have preached it without the resurrection. They would have rejected it, crushed no doubt by the necessity, but necessity there was.

2 *Nothing on which to gain a hold*

A second reason why 'it could not be that death should keep *him* (Jesus) in its grip' is because there was nothing in Jesus on which the last enemy of man could gain a hold.

This is not easy to understand at first so let me offer an illustration. Most of us will have heard of a publication called *Private Eye* even if we have never seen a copy. Its aim is to ferret out, from gossip or any other source, weak points in public figures in order to denigrate them. Usually it thinks it finds something on which to lay a hold and accomplish its purpose. This kind of destructive activity is not new. A policy of what has been called 'debunking' came into vogue in the 1920s and has never wholly ceased to operate. Almost all the great leaders of the past from John Wesley to Gladstone came in for tearing down. Warts were found and warts were magnified.

Now death is man's last enemy. Sooner or later it will bring us all down. It will work on our weaknesses, our physical weaknesses, be they of the heart, the lungs or the liver. It will work on our moral weaknesses where the sting of death lies. But what about Jesus? What were his weaknesses? What were his defects? What were his sins? If he really was the incarnate Son of God as the apostles came to proclaim and the Church came to believe, is there any sense in asking these questions of Jesus? Must we not say that they simply do not, and cannot, apply to one in whom we recognize deity? So Acts 2.24 reads *'But God raised him to life again, setting him free from the pangs of death because it could not be that death should keep him in its grip'*; there was nothing in Jesus on which death could gain a hold.

3 *Jesus is the Saviour*

And now a third point about the resurrection of Jesus we must not forget. It was not proclaimed by the apostles in their preaching as an isolated historical event. They were not out simply to put the record straight – Jesus is not dead as some people think, he rose from the dead, we saw him risen. No, they preached the resurrection of Jesus as the basis for the gospel of our salvation. Christ has died. Christ is risen. *Therefore* we are offered the gift of present and eternal salvation.

We need to grasp this. What we are offered in the person of Christ is not merely a supreme moral example, albeit a supreme example of sacrificial love to the uttermost. Nor are we offered merely a body of lofty soul-searching ethical teaching. Maybe, as they stand, these might inspire the few but they will not save the many. They may even plunge them into despair. How can ordinary mortals driven by instincts whose coarseness is most often only covered by a veneer of respectability (though occasionally exhibiting acts of heroic goodness) rise to levels of excellence such as this? What the Christian gospel offers is something different. It offers union with the risen Christ. We have it in the fourth gospel in the words of Christ himself to his disciples, *Because I live, you too will live* (John 14.19). We have it too in the words of St Paul, worth quoting at length from Romans, chapter 6 verse 8, the following: *But if we thus died with Christ* (that is gave up confidence in our sinful selves to earn the life eternal), *we believe that we shall also come to life with him. We know that Christ, once raised from the dead, is never to die again: he is no longer under the dominion of death . . . . In the same way you must regard yourselves as dead to sin and alive to God, in union with Christ Jesus.*

The key is in the closing words, *in union with Christ Jesus.* This is where our salvation is grounded, not in ourselves but in union with Christ whom death *could not keep in its grip.* Because he lives we too shall live. But how is this union effected? It is effected through faith in Christ. It is effected through self-committal to Christ. It is effected through putting ourselves on Christ's side. And even if we fall into unfaithfulness for a time, as did the disciples on Good Friday, and are penitent, he will remain faithful to us, he will hold to the union; he appeared, you will remember, that first Eastertide to the fearful, doubting, temporarily unfaithful disciples. He did not let them go. He will not let us go, however shaky our faith. So sweeping is the grace of God that even fitful faith unites to the risen Christ and brings with it the life eternal. *Because I live, you too will live.* This is the Easter gospel of the crucified, risen, Christ. This is how he is the Saviour and not merely the example or the teacher. And this is why it 'could not be that death should keep *him* in its grip'. He had to be our Saviour, we could not save ourselves.

Application

Is there at Eastertide any need to apply what all this is saying? Is not our consequent action obvious? It is to renew our union with the risen Christ and make it sure, an inward and personal disposition of mind and soul determined alone and determined in quietness. And the Church offers us a way of making that inward action more real to us and lasting, even effective; it does so with an outward and visible sign and *means* of union called the sacramant of Holy Communion. In receiving the broken bread and outpoured wine we unite ourselves in faith with the crucified and risen Christ whom 'it could not be that death should keep *him* in its grip'. What a gospel! What a source of confidence now!

> *Lord you know our weaknesses*
> > *our transgression:*
> *and our many faults.*
> *How can you not know them?*
> *But we trust in your grace,*
> > *your amazing grace,*
> > *your amazing grace in dying and rising again*
> > > *for us;*
> *So that united with you*
> > *we can rise*
> > *to newness of life today,*
> > *and courage to face tomorrow,*
> > *and a sure and certain hope of resurrection in*
> > > *the life to come.*
> *Praise be to you, Lord God,*
> *for these unspeakable gifts.*

2 Reasonable faith

John 20.8 (AV) . . . *he saw, and believed.*

1 *A necessary preamble*

This is what the fourth gospel tells us about one of the disciples of Jesus who entered the empty tomb on that first Easter morning – *he saw and believed*. This seeing and believing, however, and the context in the resurrection stories about Jesus, is precisely what a number of New Testament scholars at present find themselves unable to accept. Not that they disbelieve the resurrection of Jesus. On the contrary, they are at pains to affirm it; but they do not accept that there was any unique objective event, and certainly not an empty tomb, to evoke belief in it. What happened was that after the death and burial of Jesus those who had known him in the flesh found themselves experiencing mystical and spiritual communion with him. *Therefore* he was not dead but alive. So they sought

95

to communicate this truth of the resurrection, which is available to faith and only to faith, by means of pictures and stories. So the resurrection narratives in the four gospels are not to be read as literal accounts of what happened but as symbolic representations of spiritual truth.

This way of reading the Easter story surfaced into the general public view in 1984 and made headlines in the national press. No doubt many readers mocked, some Church people were shocked and many were puzzled. Not that it was new. Variations of it had been current in academic circles for many decades, and it was presented in a popular form by a Roman Catholic writer called H. J. Richards in his paperback first published by Collins in the Fontana series in 1976 under the title *The first Easter. What really happened?* The claim for the modern view is that it enables modern Christians to hold on to belief in the resurrection of Jesus, and removes unnecessary stumbling blocks for outsiders.

We must be careful not to question the integrity of those who take this view. If it does enable them to stay in the community of Christian faith, even to win people for it, well and good; but will it stand up to examination? Granted the resurrection narratives in the four gospels cannot be satisfactorily harmonized, granted there may be some embroidery here and there, granted no one actually saw the resurrection of Jesus take place and therefore it is not an event in the way the crucifixion was an event and so is incapable of scientific proof – still we have to ask, Was it *their faith* that caused the New Testament writers to compile these Easter stories, or was it rather that *certain unique events* caused their faith? Which way round are we to take these two? The Christian Church has traditionally taken the latter course. Some objective event or series of events *actually happened* evoking their faith in the resurrection of the Jesus who was crucified, dead and buried.

I am sorry about this rather long preamble to my simple text, *He saw and believed*, but there are times and seasons when a preacher will not be heard unless he shows himself aware of the contemporary debate perplexing a number of minds, even though he cannot in a sermon follow through the arguments for and against it.

Come back now to my text, John 20.8, *he saw and believed*. Who saw? He is called 'the other disciple', the one whom Jesus loved, usually taken to be John the apostle. The accounts says he ran with the apostle Peter early on Easter morning to the tomb where Jesus had been buried. Seeing the stone rolled back from the entrance he *peeped* in and saw the linen wrappings used in the burial lying there. Peter, ever impetuous, coming up behind went straight in and *stared* at the bare sight. (I am trying to represent in English the three different words used for 'seeing' in the Greek of this narrative.) John followed and *saw with imagination*. The linen wrappings were lying there in the grave *tidily*. Thieves do not leave a place tidy. I have been burgled more than once. I know.

The linen wrappings and anything hidden in them would be worth stealing. But they were left. They were lying there tidily. Archbishop Temple made the suggestion that the top layer was collapsed on the lower. There was a space for the neck and then the napkin or headpiece lying apart. But for these wrappings, the tomb was empty. Of John the narrative says, 'he saw and believed'. Clearly the writer wishes his readers to understand that the resurrection of Jesus, and not a case of stealing, was what he believed. This is evident from the verse (that is number 9) following. Of the other disciples it says 'until then they had not understood the scriptures, which showed that he must rise from the dead'.

Now let me make a statement and then ask a question. First the statement. As the story stands, it tells us that one follower of Jesus came to belief in the resurrection of Jesus *without* experiencing a resurrection appearance of Jesus. This is not commonly asserted nowadays, but rather that the empty tomb played no part in the resurrection faith professed by the early Church; it was the appearance of the risen Jesus to the disciples that counted. This however is not what the fourth gospel says about the beloved disciple (as he is called).

Now my question. Did the empty tomb then *prove* the resurrection of Jesus? Is it a knockdown proof? Is this what the words used of John 'he saw and believed' mean? The answer is

No. Faith never comes by way of knock-down proofs. It cannot. Faith in the resurrection of Jesus did not come to the beloved disciple this way. It came because he had known Jesus personally. Since he is called 'beloved', 'the one whom Jesus loved', we may suppose that he understood Jesus more sensitively, more intuitively, than any other in his company. Time and time again then, as he lived with Jesus, listened to him, watched him at work and at prayer, he must have wondered who he really was, wondered more than any other disciple. Was this extraordinary man from Nazareth the long-awaited Messiah? Seen in his ordinary garb it was hard to believe, but hard *not* to believe. There was something about him. Then he saw the way those linen wrappings lay in the tomb on Easter morning. Did he say to himself then – 'This is it. This is resurrection. This is that to which the scriptures bear witness. This is what Jesus himself read in the scriptures and what he had in mind when he spoke of resurrection'? If this comes anywhere near the truth we can understand, at least a little (I will not say more) the description of his experience that first Easter morning – *he saw and believed*.

3 *Believing without seeing*

Here someone may make the comment, 'All very interesting but even if true, of what value is this experience of this one man to us? We cannot see and believe. We cannot testify to any empty tomb or to any strange arrangement of burial wrappings. We have to engage with supermarkets, motorways, commuter trains and television. This is our world. As for the first Easter, all we have is four accounts of what certain persons *claimed* to have taken place, the earliest written some thirty years after the event and the latest, St John's gospel, sixty years after. And no witness was an independent one, all the evidence derives from the followers of Jesus.'

Here I have to say that very few people indeed (I am tempted to add 'if any') come to the point of belief in the resurrection of Jesus in the first place through looking up the New Testament accounts of it. We begin from our experience of Christ now. We begin from meeting the Christian spirit in a

Christian group or individual now. We begin from our reaction to the person of Jesus as he has been presented to us now – his life, his words, his wonderful works. Not until we know Christ as a reality in the present are we ready to hear that he was raised from the dead in the past and to take these resurrection narratives in the gospels seriously. Let me make the point again. John 'saw and believed' on that first Easter morning because of his prior personal experience of him.

4 *Believing is what counts*

Is there anything else to say? I think there is. These resurrection narratives in the gospels do more than confirm our personal experience, they deepen it.

Perhaps, however, the saying of Jesus at the close of the story addressed to Thomas is what will appeal to us most – *Happy are they who never saw me and yet have found faith.* This must apply to us as it applies to most of those for whom the fourth gospel was first written. How they must have rubbed their eyes to learn that they were in no way inferior to those, like the beloved disciple and Thomas, who 'saw and believed'. Nor are we. They believed. We believe. This is all that matters. It is faith that gets the Christian way of life into its stride and reaches to the eternal God through resurrection. Only faith. And by this I mean, as I am sure the New Testament means, faith based on reason, reasonable faith.

3 Angels

> Luke 24.22, 23 (NEB) '... *and now some women of our company have astounded us: they went early to the tomb, but failed to find his body, and returned with a story that they had seen a vision of angels who told them he was alive.*'

A vision of angels; this is the phrase I wish to lift out of this extract from St Luke's account of the two walking on the road to Emmaus on the evening of Easter Day. The women returned from Jesus's grave with a story that this is what they had experienced earlier in the day. It is impossible to miss the disparaging ring in the way these two travellers reported the women's story – *a vision of angels*. In their minds it gave the show away. It indicated what we might call 'a cock and bull' story. No report of any event can be taken seriously if those who present it start talking about angels. And I am afraid I have to say that the fact that they were women, emotionally disturbed women, who told the story, did not help. To the two travellers objectivity, and therefore reliability, in the reporting was doubtful.

What do you think about angels? I have to confess that for most of my life I have scarcely thought about them at all, and what little attention I have given could almost be described as 'suspended judgement', if not agnostic. Not that I could forget them altogether. For nearly twenty years I ministered in a Church where angels were depicted everywhere; carved in stone, on the tops of pillars, picked out in gold leaf on the giant ornate reredos, reaching out from the top of the organ case with long and elegant trumpets. All very satisfying aesthetically. I loved them. But what part could angels reasonably play in the faith of an intelligent Christian today? Don't they belong to the realm of the 'airy-fairy'? And then, quite recently, I turned to the New Testament expecting the references to be meagre and of no real consequence. I was astonished. I counted no less than one hundred and seventy references; fifty-one in the gospels alone, twenty-one in the Acts of the Apostles, twelve in the Epistle to the Hebrews, sixty-eight in the Apocalypse and eighteen in the rest of the New Testament writings. Can I any longer assume that the subject is only of marginal interest? I confess I have had to think again.

1 *A messenger*

What is an angel? Pared down to its basic meaning, in the Bible an angel is a messenger. To many Bible readers it comes as a surprise to learn that Malachi, the title of the last book of the Old Testament is not a proper name at all; it simply means 'my messenger' and could equally read 'my angel', as in the Greek version. If you were a Hebrew and you wanted a messenger you sent for a *Malach* and if you were a Greek you sent for an *anggelos*, which even those without a knowledge of the language can see stands for 'angel'.

So any man, any woman might be chosen by God to be his messenger, his angel to the community or to an individual. An angel was someone called to be the bearer of good tidings or the bearer or warning and judgement. An angel was not necessarily a celestial being, and certainly not with wings. All of which means, you could be an angel, so could I; we could be God's mouthpiece delivering his message: or we could be, by the way we lived, a practical example of what God wishes all his people to be. So either in speaking or by being, or in both, we could be an angel. A faint, yes very faint, echo of this truth can be heard when someone says of another who has done him or her a great kindness, 'Oh, aren't you an angel?' There is no reference to a celestial being. That person will not start sprouting wings!

2 *A hint of the supernatural*

I used to stop here – an angel is a messenger; and I can still comment – 'so far so good'. After all the angel who appeared to Mary, mother of Jesus, was God's messenger to her bearing the good tidings that she would bear a son. And the angels in the tomb on Easter morning were God's messengers bearing the good tidings that Jesus of Nazareth was risen from the grave. But there is more to it. When an angel is suddenly introduced into a New Testament story the author is saying in effect, 'Attention! Mind your step here. We have now arrived at a place where the ordinary categories of logical human reasoning no longer apply.' So in the narrative an angel provides a hint of the presence of the supernatural. It is a warning that we must come to terms with this if we are to accept the story at all.

Once grasp this and it is illuminating to observe where for instance in the story of Jesus reference is made to the presence of angels, and where it is not.

101

There is a cluster of references at the beginning, that is at the entry of Jesus into *terrestrial* life. There is also a cluster at the end, that is the entry of Jesus into *celestial* life. To put the matter another way, angels at those two points in the life of Jesus say in effect, Watch out for miracle at the birth, watch out for miracle at the death, at both these points the supernatural is pre-eminently active.

And now the places in the life of Jesus where a reference to angels is either rare or completely absent. We are told that angels ministered to him after his temptation in the wilderness at the beginning of his ministry. We are also told that an angel strengthened him in the garden of Gethsemane at the close of his ministry. For the most part however, Jesus battled with his life, as we have to battle with it, without angelic support all along the way. There was no angel present when Jesus faced the hostile crowds maddened because he would not accept their thrust to make him king after feeding the five thousand; there was no angel to help him counter the aggressive arguments of the Scribes and Pharisees bent on incriminating him before the law; there was no angel by the cross relieving the agony of his crucifixion. This is no accidental omission. It indicates that the incarnation of Jesus was real. He took the same human nature with which we are clothed. He faced life as we have to face it. He shared what we have to experience. Angels do not abound for us. They did not abound for Jesus.

And then we come to this startling fact in the New Testament. In the book of the Acts of the Apostles, which does not tell the unique story of the ministry of Jesus on earth, but rather the progress of the growth of the early church composed of people like ourselves living out our lives in a particular political and cultural setting, *angels appear again* – twelve times. So ought we to reckon with angels in the life of the Church, and in the lives of ordinary Christian people now? This is what the scriptures seem to say.

3 *Celestial beings*

And now some distinctive features about angels provided by the New Testament. They are celestial beings except for 'the angel' mentioned in some of the chapters of the Revelation where the reference seems to be to the leader of the local Church, perhaps the spirit of the congregation. Apart from this, angels are described as an innumerable host. They are the armies of heaven. This therefore is the question I have had to ask myself. 'Why should I reckon that God, who is Spirit, only created for fellowship with himself *physical* beings in space and time?' Why not spiritual beings also, inhabitants of the celestial spheres? I cannot think that we can rightly ignore such scriptures as Hebrews 12.22 . . . *you stand before Mount Zion and the city of the living God, heavenly Jerusalem, before myriads of angels, the full concourse and assembly of the first-born of the citizens of heaven*; and also this, Revelations 5.11, *Then as I looked I heard the voices of countless angels. These were all round the throne and the living creatures and the elders. Myriads upon myriads there were, thousands upon thousands*.

We are told something more about them. They are spirits, not physical bodies, and there seem to be ranks among them. They surround the throne of God and so they will accompany the Son of Man when he comes again in his glory. Their appointed task is to minister to the saints, that is God's people, not only revealing to them God's mind and will and providing on occasions assistance, but also accompanying them through the gate of death into Paradise. One of the surprising revelations is that in heaven they have a status secondary to that of the saints who have run the course of this world with faithfulness.

A sermon such as this is not the place to list all the verses in the New Testament where angels are mentioned but I cannot think of a more fascinating Bible study for anyone to undertake than to look them up with the help of a concordance. They are most illuminating.

4 *Guardian angels*

There are, however, two verses I will quote. They refer to 'guardian angels' as the New English Bible has given itself the liberty of translating the ordinary word for angel in these places.

First the words of Jesus in Matthew 18.10 about children. *Never despise one of these little ones; I tell you they have their guardian angels in heaven who look continually on the face of my heavenly Father.* Are we to understand – 'waiting for his instructions or messages'?

Then the case of St Peter (Acts 12.15) walking out of his prison where King Herod had incarcerated him in Jerusalem and knocking on the door of the house where the Christians were assembled in prayer. A maid called Rhoda was so startled on answering, that instead of letting him in, she ran to tell the assembly who it was, and they replied *You are crazy .... It must be his guardian angel.*

So have we each one a guardian angel? Let me ask a further speculative question – you might say puerile. When we come to die, will our guardian angel ease us through that fearful final gate? I confess I should like to believe this. We are of the earth, earthy. How shall we fare when we find ourselves in the celestial realms? As clumsy, awkward novices completely out of place? Let me offer an analogy. An invitation to a royal lunch party at the Palace sounds attractive. But suppose you have never been before. Where will you go? What will you say? In practice the entry is smoothed, the guests are not made to feel 'fish out of water'. A palace servant meets them at the door conducting them along the corridors, indicating exactly where to go and what to do long before they find themselves in the royal presence; and all carried out with ease and friendliness. Is this how it will be when we pass through life's final portal into the kingdom of God? Will our guardian angel function then? I do not know, but in the light of scripture I have at least the right to raise the question. Of this I am certain, this picture (if that is all it is) expresses God's care and concern for each one of us. *He knoweth our frame*, to quote the old words of scripture. He will *give grace to help in time of need.*

So in the course of speaking of angels I have come round to speak of death and resurrection, an Easter theme. I wonder now if the two travellers on the road to Emmaus, that first Easter day, were wrong to pooh-pooh the women's story of a vision of angels. I wonder if it is not at the place of dying and death that angels have a particular ministry, although unseen with the physical eye. It seems to me that however you read these scriptures there is great comfort here. God cares for us in this life. He will care for us in the life to come of which the resurrection of Jesus assures us. And he also will care for us in the solemn passage between the two realms. The angels somehow conveyed the message on that Easter morning to the women not to be afraid. Dying, if not death, is the point at which most of us are a little afraid. Therefore I derive comfort from what Hebrews 1.14 says about the angels: *they are ministrant spirits, sent out to serve, for the sake of those who are to inherit salvation.* They were sent out for our loved ones when they passed over, thank God; they will be sent out for us when our time comes.

PRAYER

> *Lord, we cannot plumb the mysteries of the eternal world,*
> *we can scarcely plumb the mysteries of this world,*
> *but we are assured that you care for us*
> *and will see us through.*

> *Lord, you have ways of helping us,*
> *ways we cannot often see,*
> *ways we cannot really comprehend,*
> *but we trust in your loving care*
> *made known in Jesus Christ*
> *for all your people,*
> *now and for ever.* *Amen.*

SIX SHORT COMPLINE ADDRESSES

1 Night-lights

In the creation narrative of Genesis, chapter 1, we read how *God made two great lights, the greater light to rule the day, and the lesser light to rule the night*. And then almost as an afterthought *he made the stars also*. The Hebrew simply reads, 'and the stars'.

Stars are visible in the darkness but they do not *shed* light, they do not light up our pathway. Nevertheless, they act as guides when everything else is black. Since the dawn of history seafarers have been dependent on the stars to maintain their course and find their way.

Sooner or later most of us undergo experiences which can only be described as darkness, sometimes thick, black darkness with no light on our path at all. We cannot see a way ahead. We may even begin to question how we shall face life. Bereavement can be such a time; or the surgeon's report that we are suffering from a malignant tumour. How can we turn up at the office with this on our mind? Or a life's partner has let us down. At such times everything comes to a standstill. We cannot even feel our way. There is no pale moonlight, let alone sunshine. Darkness reigns. Could we then remember these five words from the creation narrative? . . . *he made the stars also*.

Stars, as we see them, are mere pinpoints of light, nothing more; but by them seafarers do actually find their way. So in the dark days of our experience there will be pinpoints of light if only we will look for them. Some man, some woman, for example who did not go under experiences no less bad than ours. Some public figure who hides the fact that he is frequently attending the hospital for treatment, and going about his work as if all were well. Not much theology behind these stances! They are only pinpoints of light. Yet so are stars, but men at sea find their way by them. God made great lights, but *he made the stars also*.

Before we 'turn in' tonight and darkness reigns, let us not forget God's night time provision. When we were little children we were possibly afraid of the dark. Perhaps a tiny night-light was left by our bedside. We have grown out of this childish fear long ago. In that form, yes but does not this other fear of darkness remain compressed in the nagging worry, 'How shall I manage if . . . ?'

But God will provide. We could go to sleep tonight with this reassurance. 'He made the stars also.' Perhaps we cannot always see the stars, not when the sky is overcast or it is thick with clouds; but they are still there. They will be visible again before many nights are gone. We shall not for long be bereft of direction how to proceed *whatever happens*. God has seen to that. *He made the stars also.*

2 If only . . .

It has been pointed out that *if only* Kaiser Wilhelm I who was made Emperor at Versailles in 1871 had not lived till he was ninety-one, Kaiser Frederick III would have come to power. He, with his liberal ideas, supported by his wife Victoria, would have ousted Bismark. Then Bismark's military Prussianism, together with the flamboyant William II would not have led Germany into a position where war became inevitable. If only William I, a good if limited man, had died at a normal age instead of ninety-one Europe might have been saved the terror of World War One and its equally terrible consequences.

If only . . . . There are some things we simply do not understand, not even in the light of Faith in God. Our religion does not light up the whole of our past nor the whole of our future. What it does is to give us sufficient light for the next step ahead. All of which means that it is nothing more than a pointless game to wonder what might have happened *if only* . . . .

There must be many individuals tempted to look back in their own personal history and wonder *if only* . . . . It is a waste of time. The right course is to rise up and tackle the immediate task. Our eyes must be on what is, not on what might have been. God gives us sufficient light for each day if we ask him.

This will be true of our tomorrow. None of us knows exactly how it will turn out, but we can go to bed now, knowing that God will not have forsaken us when we have gone to sleep. This is the reassuring thought about the God and Father of our Lord Jesus Christ that even if we forget him, he will not forget us; if we make a mess of tomorrow he will not wash his hands of us; the New Testament tells us that, should it be that we become faithless (horrible thought!), he will abide faithful. We are safe with God. We can rub out the haunting little phrase 'if only' and not waste any more time on it, and certainly not keep awake because of it when we could be properly asleep.

God will never leave nor forsake us.

3 Forgiveness

After the end of the war in 1945 a German interned in Denmark, wretched with hunger and the separation from his people, received a surprise invitation from a Danish family completely unknown to him. Mystified, he nevertheless called at the house and was still more surprised to see the living room gaily decorated and the table richly laid. Was this really all for him? Apparently it was. The householder warmly invited him to take his place. When the meal was over however he spoke of the death of his son whom Germans had killed. 'Today,' he said, 'is the anniversary of his death'. The German internee expected expressions of bitter hatred to follow. But no, nothing followed, except a pleasant goodbye when it was time for the German to return to his prison camp. Then it dawned on him. He could scarcely believe it. This Danish couple had invited him to their home, given him their son's place at table in order to offer him as the representative of the whole German people – even his son's murderers – their forgiveness. Because they lived by God's forgiveness they felt they could not refuse it to others.

We hardly know what to make of this story which I have translated from a German source, but it is true. We have repeated, however, in our prayers tonight the Lord's Prayer with the petition *Forgive us our trespasses as we forgive those who trespass against us* or, as the NEB has it at Matthew 6.12 *Forgive us the wrong we have done, as we have forgiven those who wronged us*.

But have we? Perhaps we have been wronged in the last twelve hours since last we went to bed. Shall we be lying down tonight nursing resentment if not hatred? This is not a good way to prepare for sleep. It is better for us to let our anger die down with the sun and leave all the vengeance for God to repay if he wishes to do so. And he may. There is nothing like a heart and mind at rest with God and with our fellow men and women as a prelude to sleep whatever may have happened to disturb us in the last twelve hours.

I expect the Danish couple slept that night when they went to bed, and the German had returned to his camp. Perhaps he slept too. He scarcely thought such peace possible in this torn world.

4 Sleep

Psalm 3.5 *I laid me down and slept, and rose up again: for the Lord sustained me.*

Who is this who goes to bed, sleeps soundly and wakes in the morning thoroughly refreshed? Some thick-skinned, insensitive creature who 'drops off' like an animal without a care for the next moment, let alone the next day? But he writes poetry! Poetry up to the standard of Psalm 3! Some lucky man then who hasn't a care in the world and whose life flows by as in some Elysian fields? But he begins his poem, 'Lord, how increased are they that trouble me: many are they that rise against me. Many there be that say of my soul: there is no help for him in his God.'

Most of us have had some experience of sleepless nights. We have gone over and over tomorrow's problems in our minds. We have got up, paced the room, regretted that the night is only half through, taken another sleeping tablet, then dozed off only to wake more weary in the morning than when we went to bed.

109

I wonder if Jesus ever found it impossible to sleep? We read that the night before his crucifixion his disciples slept 'like logs', but he wrestled in an agony of fear. But in his prayer he regained his poise. Is this how it always was with him? Had he our frailties as well as our strengths, but in his case the frailties were mastered through self-committal into the hands of a caring Father? Did he in the first place learn this secret from Psalm 3 which he must have known from a child, and later came to understand and apply? After all, the Psalter was his prayer book. He read, *I did call upon the Lord with my voice: and he heard me out of his holy hill. I laid me down and slept, and rose up again: for the Lord sustained me. I will not be afraid for ten thousands of the people: that have set themselves against me round about.*

We are not all made alike. Some are placid, some are nervous. Sleep is an index of the kind of persons we are. Is it also an index of the kind of faith we exercise? This is an awkward question and we try to dodge it. Perhaps we ought to rub out Psalm 3 as hopelessly naïve. Would this be right? I don't think it would be right. Yes, we have experienced sleepless nights, but we have also experienced the Lord's sustaining power. This is the message of the psalm for us. God sustains those who trust him. We need reminding of this over and over again for we constantly slip back into the old routine of worry.

Let this be our last thought tonight when we put out the light. Faith in God's sustaining power can act like food and drink to us. It enables us to keep going even when the odds seemed stacked against us.

5 The burglar

> Luke 12.39 (NEB) *And remember, if the householder had known what time the burglar was coming he would not have let his house be broken into.*

This is the trouble with burglars, they do not announce the time of their arrival. The reasons are obvious. The reasons are

110

also obvious why we all wish to keep the burglars out. What is not so obvious is why Jesus of Nazareth, who said this, implied that God acts like a burglar, and why we as householders are anxious above all else to keep him out.

What happens is that life, or a great deal of it anyway, apparently goes on as if God were not involved. He seems to take no obvious part in the conduct of affairs. He is the absent God, the *Deus absconditus*. We might perhaps at one time, possibly years ago, have thought of God as actually intervening. One or two startling turns of events in our experience led us to think this way. But waiting for such drastic events to occur again became unreasonable. Moreover, waiting is a boring business. So we get on with organizing our lives without God. We construct our own programmes, set up our ideologies, and even make forecasts about the future. With all these securities around us like a house, anyone breaking in and upsetting them, not least God himself, would be like a burglar coming. It is definitely not what we want.

Perhaps today has been like this. We knew exactly what we were going to do. The diary was made up, the appointments fixed. There was the shopping to be done, the children to fetch. The time schedule was tight. The last thing we wanted was for our programme to be thrown out, but it was, it was like a burglar breaking in and upsetting everything.

But God sometimes does this. He breaks into our programme like a burglar. An illness attacks. An accident occurs. A visitor appears on the doorstep begging our help. Our train is cancelled. If only these events would not occur when we least want them or expect them.

Before we go to sleep tonight could we make a mental effort to rid ourselves of any lingering resentment at what has happened today, or the other day? Could we bring our minds round to recognizing that *God* may have been involved in the intrusion?

I can tell you what one of the results would be because I have gone through this kind of resentment quite often. When I have remembered that God might be the burglar of my diary I have quietened down. And that is a very good thing to do before you go to bed.

6 Ballast

It was not until I read it somewhere the other day that I understood how in a way our lives are like ships at sea, cargo ships. Their *raison d'etre* is that they shall arrive safe at their destination port with their cargo intact. So on their way across the ocean it is essential that they float well down in the water. If too much hull is exposed severe danger from wind and waves is likely. Therefore if the cargo is insufficient the ship takes on ballast to keep it down. What it must not do is attempt to skim along the surface. The sea may get rough.

God in his mercy and foreknowledge often weighs us down with burdens, sorrows and disappointments. Without them we should be light-hearted people only fit for sailing in fair weather. The ballast in our lives is there so that we shall come safely to port. We are at risk without ballast. We must be careful how we complain about it.

There is also this to remember. God does not *overload* his ships. He does not weigh us down so that we sink under the weight of what he gives us to carry. No shipowner would ever dream of doing so. God does not tempt us, says St Paul, beyond what we can bear, and with the temptation he always provides a way of escape.

These are thoughts to turn over at the end of the day. Perhaps one way or another we have carried quite a load in the last twelve hours. Could we think of it as ballast? And could we remember that God wishes above all else that we shall arrive intact at our final destination? With this in mind he provides ballast, but not too much.

A QUIET DAY

1 Petitionary Prayer

Luke 11.9 (NEB) *Ask, and you will receive.*

My subject for this quiet day is prayer, not corporate prayer, nor liturgical prayer but private prayer, the kind of prayer we engage in on our own, or don't engage in, because we find it too difficult, or reckon it childish. And I am going to limit myself even further, I am going to speak about petitionary prayer, the kind of prayer disturbingly implied by Jesus's words in Luke 11, *And so I say to you, ask, and you will receive; seek, and you will find; knock, and the door will be opened.* There are times when we all wish to retort 'Will it?' Will the doors of heaven be opened to my prayers?

1 *Petitionary prayer has a rightful place*

I know of course that petitionary prayer is by no means the sum total of prayer. Poor indeed would be the quality of the relationship between a son and a father if it never extended beyond the son's asking for things. And the same applies to our relationship with the heavenly Father. No, there is praise and thanksgiving; and prayer ought not to proceed without them. There is also penitential prayer when we confess our sins. We have 'got ourselves all wrong' if we reckon that we are such splendid creatures we need not be involved in confession at all. And at the opposite extreme from asking there is listening, or if you like 'waiting on God'. Reading the Bible prayerfully could rightly belong to this part of prayer. And there is simply being in the presence of God, still and receptive. It is quite likely that we do not have enough silence in our times of prayer both corporate and private.

My wife and I have often had fun in a restaurant looking round at the other couples at the other tables and trying to guess which of them could be classified as married. We came to the conclusion that they were at the tables where there was no animated and ceaseless conversation filling up every minute with words. No, not because these couples were bored with each other as the marriage cynics would say but because they were happy simply to be in each other's presence, they were out together.

Prayer can consist of simply being in God's presence. Prayer is certainly not wholly accomplished by asking God for things, but the point I wish to make is that it is not improper to do so. Petitionary prayer has a rightful place in prayer. We can ask, we can seek, we can knock. I would go so far as to say we have not reached the heart of prayer as Jesus understood if we leave it out altogether for whatever reasons.

I was struck the other day in reading the First Epistle to Timothy in the Greek Testament by the words in chapter 2, *First of all, then, I urge that petitions, prayers, intercessions, and thanksgiving be offered for all men.* It was the third word which took hold of me, the word for intercessions. It only occurs here and in chapter 4 of this letter, and nowhere else in the New Testament. It is a strange word *enteuchseis* deriving from the verb *entugchano* which means to go along and meet somebody in order to converse with them. What a friendly, almost familiar, way this is to describe prayer! But from the gospel accounts it looks as if Jesus understood prayer in this intimate fashion. He saw it and practised it in terms of a child happily going off to talk to his father.

2 *Embarrassment about petitionary prayer*

(a) Perhaps we find ourselves embarrassed by this kind of intimacy and personal approach. It is too down to earth, too ordinary. What we prefer is some form of mystical approach which may take the form of meditation. There has been a considerable growth in this area of religious awareness in recent years encouraged to some extent by contacts with eastern religious practice. We can be thankful for this awareness of the spiritual dimension of human existence, the lack of which is so detrimental to the wholesomeness of the secularized and materialistic West, paralysed in its affluence. But there is a price to pay if the mystical/meditative approach is counted as the whole of prayer with no intercession in it. It results in,

114

indeed it aims at, the absorption of the individual in the great mystic absolute in which my desires, my failings, my fears are lost in the infinite. With this kind of prayer there is frequently some form of asceticism in order to bring the body into subjection to the absorption process. We can be certain that Jesus was happy simply to be in the Father's presence and this was prayer, but it does not appear that anything like mysticism in the form of absorption into the infinite was his understanding of it.

(b) Perhaps we are embarrassed by the supposed unscientific assumptions of petitionary prayer. What is the trouble? We may express it in the form of a question. Does not nature work according to fixed laws? And must it not be so? Where should we be if fire did not *always* burn, and water *always* drown? And does not our religion actually require this unbreakable regularity? If God created the world, must he not have created the laws which govern its consistent working? Not even God then can suspend the operation of natural law, whether we pray or not? So we sing

> *Laws, which never shall be broken,*
> *For their guidance he hath made.*
>
> (*Foundling Hospital Collection 1796*)

But wait a minute. Is nature all so neatly tied up? What about the operation of chance? What about the part it plays in evolution? A learned book has just been written to show how God makes use of chance in his method of operation. Or again do not the physicists tell us of a principle of indeterminacy at the heart of the matter? Leaving these two observations aside let us look a little more closely to see what these laws of nature are. They are deductions from the scientist's classification of what he observes. Classification means putting in a class together all that is seen to possess similar characteristics. It is not surprising then that all that is classified reacts similarly. But what if something could be found so individual that it could not be subject to classification? Would not the universality of what are called 'laws', though widely applicable, have reached a point where it did *not* apply. And such individuality does exist in the human person. Human beings can indeed be classified up to a point. They have two eyes, two legs, one mouth and so on, but no two persons are *exactly* alike. There are no copies and no repeats of persons. The marvel of the human being is that in him individuality reigns supreme. At this point classification has reached its limit and so *at the same point* so-called universal laws have reached their limit.

None of the foregoing proves the power of prayer but it does ask if we are right to reject it on the grounds that it is unscientific.

(c) We have not however quite finished with the doubts concerning petitionary prayer. Is this kind of prayer necessary? Does not God not only know all about us but also know what is best for us? Or again, is not petitionary prayer impious? Is it not based on supposition that we can properly seek to alter the will of God? But can we? Does not spiritual maturity rest in coming to the point of accepting what is as somehow in the purpose of a caring heavenly Father? So we find even such a giant of a preacher as F. W. Robertson of Brighton (1816–53) telling his hearers that they should pray until they reached the mature spiritual stage of not needing to pray at all; then they would simply accept in faith what God wills. And suppose we do not go to these lengths, suppose we still take part in intercessions in our worship, intercessions on behalf of other people, those in need and those caught up in the world's calamities, is it that we do not look to God to alter situations, but that what we are doing is putting ourselves in the presence of God so that *our* wills, *our* energies, and *our* expertise will be stirred up to go out and work for the improvement of those situations which trouble us?

3 Reassurance about petitionary prayer

Perhaps we can sum up all these doubts and difficulties about prayer by saying that we reckon that there are situations in which it is useless to pray. There is a story about the Duke of Cambridge, George IV's younger brother, who had a habit of speaking aloud his private thoughts in church. Once, at a time of drought, when the vicar was praying earnestly for rain the Duke was overheard to mutter, 'No good, no good at all, not

116

while the wind remains in the north east'. Presumably he did not reckon that God either could or would change the wind to the south west.

We do, however, set a limit to our prayers. When a man has had a leg amputated, no one asks God to make a new one grow overnight, or ever! So we cannot in this whole consideration of petitionary prayer throw reason to the winds; but the point I wish to make is that the considerations to which we have given our attention are not such as to make petitionary prayer unreasonable even though its basis is faith. We need not, we ought not to throw it away as an unreasonable, childish and naïve activity accomplishing nothing.

So we may take Luke, chapter 11, seriously. It is all about prayer, at least *nearly* all of it; more, certainly, than we at a first glance see. It begins, *Once, in a certain place, Jesus was at prayer. When he ceased, one of his disciples said, 'Lord, teach us to pray, . . .'.* And before we know where we are we have what is called the Lord's Prayer with a petition in it, a petition concerning something than which there is nothing more ordinary, nothing more material, 'Give us each day our daily bread'. And in the next breath (as Luke has arranged his material) Jesus capped it with a story of a man in such a predicament that he hammered on a door at midnight pressing a petition for three loaves of bread, yes, as precise as that, *three* loaves; and this is followed by the challenging exhortation arising out of it, even authoritatively emphasized with the words, *And so I say to you, – ask, and you will receive; seek, and you will find; knock, and the door will be opened.* Nor is this all, as you will observe if you use the time on this quiet day between the addresses to study this chapter 11.

You will discover, if you take my advice, that God does not cheat people who pray; and you will see that Luke has seen fit to attach a miracle healing story to this section on prayer suggesting the connection between Jesus's prayer and Jesus's power. There was opposition to this connection on the part of some of the people as there still is today. Prayer definitely is not, according to them, instrumental in accomplishing healing. There is no possibility of the finger of God being brought into action to accomplish such marvels. Can we be neutral in

117

the matter? Apparently not. Either we are for or against. So the words of Jesus in verse 23.

Perhaps this exegesis has proceeded far enough to open up the subject of petitionary prayer as presented by St Luke, and thereby to encourage us in the practice of petitionary prayer. Clearly Jesus expected situations to be altered as a result of such prayer, and not merely the minds of the petitioners. Let me emphasize again that petitionary prayer is not the whole of prayer but is a proper part of it. It is not contrary to reason. It is not childish. We can *let our requests be made known to God* and there is more to the practice than psychological therapy. God hears and God answers. Listen to the words of Jesus again as St Luke has presented them: 'And so I say to you, ask, and you will receive; seek, and you will find; knock, and the door will be opened. For everyone who asks receives, he who seeks finds, and to him who knocks, the door will be opened.' If this were not so God would be inferior to the laziest man we know, and the most deceitful. This in effect is what Jesus said. Do look at St Luke, chapter 11.

2 Praying in Faith

> Mark 9. 23 (RSV) *All things are possible to him who believes.*

In the first of this group of three addresses I sought to defend and encourage petitionary prayer referring to it in the plain language of 'praying for things'. I said it was not the whole of prayer, but Christian prayer, prayer after the pattern of what Christ taught, keeps it at the heart of prayer.

1 *A humble approach*

I ought to expand this a little, and for two reasons. One is that it might appear from this employment of this somewhat loose phrase – praying for things – that we can approach God with

118

a kind of shopping list: 'I want this, I want that.' Why not include a Rolls Royce? or a trip to the Bahamas! And the other reason is this – since such an idea is too puerile for serious consideration, the whole idea of petitionary prayer might be rejected altogether.

So I remind you of two events recorded in St John's gospel which put petitionary prayer in its proper perspective. In chapter 2. 1–11, at the wedding feast in Cana of Galilee, the mother of Jesus said to him, 'They have no wine left'. And in chapter 11.3, the two sisters of Lazarus, Mary and Martha, at Bethany, sent him a message saying, 'Sir, you should know that your friend lies ill'. The women on each occasion petitioned Jesus. At Cana the mother of Jesus prayed for more wine. (This was the implication of what she said.) And at Bethany the two sisters prayed for the recovery of their brother. (This was the implication of their message.) In neither situation did the women retreat for meditation, nor did they ask that their wills might be brought into line with the will of God in permitting the illness. No, they *asked for things*. They requested Jesus to make good a deficiency of material substance and to recover a man from sickness. But note how these petitioners made no demands in their petitions, all they did was to mention their concerns in his presence. Notice too, that they made no suggestions as to how he should meet their worries and they certainly did not go on and on. And observe, in the third place, that what was in their minds was not luxuries but help in situations of alarming need, and that not directly their own. There is no suggestion of 'shopping list prayer' here, and no semblance of any kind of prayer pressure.

But there was confidence that such personal and domestic concerns could properly be brought to their Lord. And there was faith that he both could and would deal with their troubled situation, but in his own way and in his own time. This is brought out by the fact that at Cana Jesus did not answer his mother's request forthwith, and at Bethany he both delayed his answer and allowed the situation to deteriorate before he acted. All of which should remind us to keep our place when we pray, because the heavenly Father to whom we make our petitions is the almighty Lord, and we are no more than his

119

humble servants. He will meet our needs but in his own way and in his own time.

It would appear from these two events in the fourth gospel and from the various requests made for the healing of sick persons in the synoptic gospels that petitionary prayer is always and exclusively for some basic need to be met. It is not for plenty, it is only for necessity. The petition in the Lord's Prayer appears to look the same way – *Give us this day our daily bread*. Are we to suppose then that God is only interested so long as we grub along just above the bread line? I do not think so. There is a text in Proverbs 10.22, memorable in the old form of words, which reads, *The blessing of the Lord, it maketh rich, and he addeth no sorrow with it*. And Psalm 65 reads (BCP version) *Thou crownest the year with thy goodness: and thy clouds drop fatness*. We ought not to underrate the blessing of God on a life. We ought never to question his generosity. God is no 'skinflint'. As the writer of the letter to Timothy put it (1 Timothy 6.17), *He gives us richly all things to enjoy*. So we can go cheerfully to pray. God gives more than we ask or think, desire or deserve.

2 *Approach with faith*

From what I have said already it should be evident that faith is the basic requirement in prayer, faith of course that God actually exists. There is no sense in praying to a God who is not there or is absent or dead. Atheists do not consciously pray. Why should they? Prayer necessitates belief in a God present now. And not only present but that he responds to those who seek him, two points made nowhere more succinctly than in Hebrews 11.6 . . . *anyone who comes to God must believe that he exists and that he rewards those who search for him*.

There is however another consideration regarding faith. God does not, indeed cannot (so it seems) work without it. I take my cue from Our Lord. We are told in Mark 6.5 and 6 that, on his return to his home town Nazareth, *he could work no miracle there, except that he put his hands on a few sick people and healed them; and he was taken aback at their lack of faith*. And in Matthew 17.19, 20 we read of his disciples enquiring the

120

reason for their failure to heal an epileptic boy. The answer given was, *Your faith is too weak*, which was immediately and emphatically elaborated as follows, *I tell you this: if you have faith no bigger even than a mustard-seed, you will say to this mountain, 'Move from here to there!', and it will move; nothing will prove impossible for you.*

'Moving mountains' is a *pictorial* way of making a point. No one would contemplate it literally. But the phrase has entered into our everyday speech to describe accomplishing the apparently impossible. We talk about mountains of work, mountains of problems, mountains of difficulties. They appear unable ever to be shifted. 'But no', says Jesus in effect, 'they can be moved, and faith in God is the instrument for doing it.'

Note the phrase 'doing it'. Faith does not mean sitting down in the belief that the mountain will move itself if we have the right attitude of mind towards it. We have to gird up our loins and work; but not work without faith in God's power at work with us while we work. *Laborare est orare* – working is praying – is incorrect. *Laborare et orare* – praying and working – is the right way, that is, praying in faith. For this is what faith does, it opens up the personality to the Spirit of God, and the Spirit of God is the power of God. When we open up to God in prayer with faith we are empowered to achieve the otherwise impossible. We remove mountains.

Christian history is scattered with examples of this. Let one suffice. On 4 July 1845, there was born a baby boy called Thomas John. He was so puny the doctor declared he had only the barest chance of survival. But he did survive. Then at the age of two he fell desperately ill. The same doctor was called in and pronounced him dead. The next day when the little body was to be placed in his coffin the parents suddenly stopped. 'His heart is still beating', they cried. They had not the slightest doubt that God had given them back their child. But why? What had God in prospect for him? No one could foresee what in fact happened. This same Thomas John Barnardo grew up and qualified as a doctor. After which, working night after night, year in and year out, carrying a lantern he sought out the homeless children under the arches and in the alleyways of the desperately poverty stricken quarters of London. He saved thousands upon thousands accommodating them in homes. The work goes on still after a hundred years, and in many more cities than London. Dr Barnardo moved mountains *by* his work, yet not by work alone, but by work and faith in the enabling power of God, for he was a committed Christian.

It is at the point of faith that we touch upon the weakness of what may loosely be described as rationalism in religion. Not that it has no wish to win adherents for the Christian way of life, not that it is wrong to apply reason to religion, for it is proper to do so. The cause why, by and large, the rationalistic approach to religion is defective as an agent for spreading the Christian gospel is that in its fear of credulity it has been over-cautious about faith. Unwelcome to some ears as it may sound, it appears from Christian history that over-belief is more effective than under-belief, though it were well if both extremes could be avoided. The failure of Our Lord's disciples to cure the epileptic boy (reported in all three synoptic gospels) through lack of faith stands as a warning to us all, not least to academic theologians.

Here then is the lesson. When we pray, we must believe that God will help us in our work to move mountains.

3 *The community of faith*

My third point is this. We need, all of us, to belong to a praying community. I am not referring to a specially convened prayer group, though this can be most helpful when it can be had. I am referring to membership in the Church as opposed to isolated and individual personal prayer. This latter ought to be. Do not misunderstand me. But there ought also to be, behind the individual Christian and round about the individual Christian at prayer, the praying Church.

I have been impressed in reading of Michael Bordeaux's work at Keston College in Kent where up-to-date and reliable information is kept about Christians in Russia. Apparently what helps to sustain them in their lonely witness is the knowledge that the Church in the West constantly remembers them in prayer.

This is the point I wish to make. Our individual faith waxes and wanes. Sometimes it is so strong it will remove mountains. At other times it is so feeble it is almost non-existent. This is what we have to remember, that in our times of faith-weakness God will come to our aid just as if we had faith-strength *because* we belong to the community of faith, the believing Church. This could be expressed another way by saying that the believing Church carries with it into the presence of God the individual person whose faith has fallen into weakness. Faith saves. Over and over again Jesus said so in so many words. And the faith of the Church saves. It is good to know that when our faith is paralysed by what has befallen us, or as a result of some tragic occurrence in the world around us, we may, like the paralytic in the story recorded in St Mark, chapter 2, be *carried* by other believing people into the presence of the healing Christ who responds to their faith so meeting our needs.

So stay in the believing community. Some day you may need to be carried by caring people when you fall down on your faith. And if you never do fall down (what an unusual person you must be!) then your steadfast faith will be helping to carry others in desperate need or in grim isolation like those brave Christian men and women in the Soviet Union today. Your faith will help to save them.

And Jesus said . . .
'All things are possible to him who believes.'
I believe, help my unbelief.

Mark 9.33 and 24

3 Praying as best you can

In this third address on prayer I wish to be practical, even 'down to earth', which is why I have given it the title 'praying as best you can'. I recognize that for most of you your time is anything but your own. You live under some degree of pressure whether in your work, or in your domestic responsibilities, or by reason of a combination of both. And for many people there is a tedious commuter journey each day, making for an early start and quite a late home coming. Some men never see their gardens in daylight throughout the whole winter except at weekends. To some extent it is this pressure and this overcrowding of time that makes a quiet day like this welcome, but it also throws up into prominence an awkward question, how we can possibly fit prayer into our normal and regular crammed schedule.

1 *Time*

I suggest that the first requirement is to settle the time of our private prayer. No rule can be laid down for everyone because situations and opportunities vary.

I was sitting in recently with a group of men and women studying for a non-stipendiary ministry. And if anybody knows the meaning of a packed life these people do, trying to hold down a job and to be students at the same time. We were listening to a godly woman describing her method of private prayer. She sits up in bed and operates a system of cards on which she has written the needs of different people and different good causes that have come to her attention. Holding the cards one by one she makes the subject written thereon a matter of sincere and concentrated intercessory prayer. Splendid! But she is retired, a little frail and lives alone. So I was not surprised to overhear the man sitting next to me mutter to himself, 'No good for me! No good at all! I'd just fall asleep! I guess I should too, but that is neither here nor there. The point is, we each have to find our own way.

Consider then this question of time. It needs to be when we can be reasonably sure of not being disturbed. This rules out the early morning for many people. Starting the day is usually a bit of a scramble. There is the breakfast to prepare, albeit there isn't often eggs and bacon these days. There are the children to get off to school. There is that commuter train to catch which waits for nobody. Ideally no doubt we should rise half-an-hour earlier and keep that 'morning watch', as it used to be called, but it isn't easy, if even possible in a family under modern living conditions. So we must find another time.

For housewives I suggest the middle of the morning when it is possible and legitimate to sit down for fifteen minutes with a cup of coffee. This could be the prayer time. For men and women in business something in the lunch hour might be appropriate. An opportunity for quite a number of people, I discovered, is provided by the train or bus journey. Apart from possible, perhaps probable, jostling, you will not be disturbed. You can even close your eyes. People will simply conclude you have gone to sleep. I first encountered this idea during the war when a member of my congregation in London who had no peace in his flat (so I guessed) used the time he had to stand each day on the half-hour bus journey rumbling into Camden Town. He was a fitter engaged on war work. The overriding necessity whatever time is chosen is that you should be alone, alone with God. I am quite sure that when our Lord lived in that tiny house in Capernaum at the beginning of his Galilean ministry – and remember the whole family plus the lodger (Jesus) would occupy the one room – he rose early and went up into the hills to pray, because only so could he be alone with God. Perhaps I ought to add this. We must stick to our time each day. Regularity is important. Each day at about the same time there ought to be that little retreat. Five minutes, ten minutes, fifteen minutes – whatever is possible.

2 Place

And now place. At first this sounds unrealistic. Most of us do not live in palaces or historic houses with a private chapel attached. And most of us are unable to make our way to the parish church each day. A church, however, does provide the opportunity to have this as a place for prayer for some. In the City of London it is quite astonishing to see how many men 'drop in' to a church after leaving their train or bus, and before entering the office, with the express purpose of having their ten minutes of private prayer undisturbed. Where this is not possible a seat in the park might suffice. I have already mentioned the train itself or the bus as a place for prayer.

For those whose private praying can be done at home, and there is much to be said for this, there is value in always using the same chair set in the same position, so that we can say to ourselves, 'This is my *place* of prayer'. Somehow this helps to cause praying to become fixed in the midst of a busy routine.

I was impressed, when I noticed, in Acts, chapter 16, how at sea Paul and Barnabas felt in the bustling city of Philippi *till they found a place of prayer*. They were there on the second evangelistic tour; but how start, how accomplish anything in a great Roman colony such as this city was? What they needed first of all was a prayer base, and they found it down by the river where women gathered for prayer. It was from this place that the work developed and grew into the church of Philippi, to which subsequently Paul wrote one of his happiest letters; we have it in the New Testament.

It looks as if Jesus had a place of prayer in Judaea, namely the garden of Gethsemane, or an 'enclosed plot of ground' as the Greek text has it. Notice the word 'enclosed', suggesting its relative privacy, a place where one could be undisturbed. Apparently Jesus often resorted to it from the hustle and bustle of Jerusalem. He went there the night before his crucifixion. Judas went there too, with the arrest party. He knew where the Master he was about to betray could be found, in his place of prayer.

Maybe not many of us are fortunate enough to possess a garden; anyway not a garden where we are not overlooked. I have one now, and in the summer months a stone seat in it (with a cushion!) is my place of prayer; but for many years the only regular praying I could do in the open air was in Kensington Gardens. I commend open-air praying. It can open up the personality to the greatness and grandeur of the creator who is also our Father. Try when you are on holiday in the summer. Walk along the deserted beach before breakfast and say the Te Deum out loud, or better still, sing it. The seagulls won't mind.

And now tools for praying. I shall mention five, the fifth rather different from the other four. In so far as we are considering the practice of prayer, I do not wish to list these in any order of priority. They all need to be available together. And what I suggest is that you have a few inches on a bookshelf, or space in a drawer where you keep these tools together; and if possible, let it be near your place of prayer. I say 'if', because obviously you will not be able to have it near you in a bus or commuter train!

You ought to have a Bible. It is not for me to recommend which version you use; the Authorized or Revised are more memorable from a literary point of view, and there is value in this. The modern translations on the other hand often help with the meaning, especially in the letters of St Paul. You will use the Bible in prayer in order to listen to God speaking to you instead of you speaking to God. Therefore, as you read have a question on your lips, 'What does this scripture say to me today?' Next I will mention the Book of Psalms, preferably the form to which you are accustomed in worship. It is worth remembering that the Psalms constituted Jesus's prayer book. He even quoted from them in his dying hours. Doubtless he was brought up on them. They were part of his devotional life. You will find almost everything you need for prayer in the Psalms. There is praise, petition and complaint, and much else besides. All our varying moods seem to be covered. You really will be praying with Christ if you use the Psalms. You will be using the forms God will hear.

A third tool is a hymn book. I find the mention of this comes as a surprise to many people. They had never thought of using hymns for prayers. Perhaps it is time we learned this lesson from the German Lutheran Church where the *Gesangbuch* means a great deal in individual piety. Read as prayers some of the hymns you know well and love. You may even discover that you had never really noticed the words before. Let me choose a hymn almost at random.

> *At thy feet, O Christ, we lay*
> *Thine own gift of this new day;*

Doubt of what it holds in store
Makes us crave thine aid the more;
Lest it prove a time of loss,
Mark it, Saviour, with thy Cross.   (*W. Bright*)

It is number 6 in *Hymns Ancient and Modern Revised*, but they have been using it in Germany at least since 1695 when it was published. I say therefore, possess a hymn book and use it for praying.

And now books of prayers. Their number is almost legion and it would be unwise of me to mention any particular titles. But I recommend using such a book not least because our own prayers tend to stay on an elementary level and almost die in a rut. You will find a selection of such books in any religious bookshop and it is worth buying just one. When you have worn it out, I don't mean literally, buy a different one. This serves as a way to keep one's prayers fresh and also to broaden and deepen them.

And now my fifth tool, rather different as I have already said. This is your memory. Memorize some prayers. Learn by heart some of the collects from the Book of Common Prayer or the Alternative Service Book. I take it you know the Lord's Prayer by heart. You should know a few others as well. The day will come when you are ill. You will neither be able to read prayers or compose prayers. You will be glad then that you are able to breathe some prayers. This is how Jesus prayed on the cross. And it is possible, though I hope it will never happen to you, that you are cut off from all facilities to use any tools in prayer. You will be sustained if you can employ this tool of memory.

I am not sure that I am the right person to give this address on prayer, because I am such a long way from being a master of the art. I cannot sustain long sessions of prayer as some do. On the other hand, I may even be exactly the right person, being close to most ordinary people in this respect. I know in myself the urge to pray and I know in myself the difficulties. So what I have done is share with you my experience in the hope that it will encourage you along this necessary path of Christian discipleship. We must never be content with talking

128

about God, no, not even if we are theologians. We must also talk *to* God and listen. Without prayer our Christian life will not be sustained.

A LEADERSHIP COURSE

1 Pitfalls for leaders

In considering this subject of leadership I ought at the outset to make two introductory points. First, what I shall say has a primary reference to leadership in the Church, but it is not without application in a wider field. Secondly, to point out the importance attached to the leadership principle in the Bible. In the economy of God the method employed to rescue, remake and re-equip communities and individuals is not by theories of existence, philosophies or even theologies but through persons who act as leaders. Indeed the Bible can be read as the record of a chain of leaders – Abraham, Moses, Joshua, Deborah (yes, a woman!), Samson (can you believe it?), Samuel, then the kings and the prophets, till there comes the *archegos*, the pioneering leader of our salvation. And even after him the chain continues with St Paul, and outside the New Testament altogether a long line of saints, martyrs, evangelists and reformers. God brings his people home by means of people.

But there are pitfalls in the leadership principle. The most obvious are tyranny and autocracy. Germany in this century ran into them in a terrible way with its elevation of the *Führerprinzip*. I doubt if the danger lies here for modern church leadership; the influence of the democratic principle is far too widespread.

1 *Standoffishness*

What then are the pitfalls? Standoffishness is one. No one likes the sound of it but it is the most excusable trap into which a leader can fall. He wishes to be impartial, and rightly so. No blue-eyed boys for him who can do no wrong. Added to this he stands off for safety's sake. Don't blame him. Every leader has to be careful. There are people ready to manipulate him. So he stands apart. He is friendly to all but friends of none. And the result? He is accused of standoffishness.

Before you roundly condemn this leader, let me remind you

that there was a certain stand-apartness with Jesus. Listen to Mark 9.32, *But they did not understand what he said, and were afraid to ask him*; and to this in 10.32, *They were on the road, going up to Jerusalem, Jesus leading the way; and the disciples were filled with awe; while those who followed behind were afraid*; and this in John 21.12, that remarkable post-resurrection story of Jesus inviting the disciples to breakfast which he had cooked (well, read the story!), *None of them dared ask 'Who are you', knowing it was the Lord*. Clearly there was a certain gap between the leader and the led in the case of Jesus and his followers for which there was a healthy respect. Jesus exhibited a certain stand-apartness.

Is the answer to our problem to be found here? The twelve had not chosen Jesus to be their leader. There was no democratic principle at work in the apostolic circle. Nor were the twelve elected by the main body of Jesus's followers. They were chosen *by Jesus*. For all that his leadership was not imposed. The disciples did not *feel* it was imposed. On the contrary, they accorded him leadership because they recognized that he stood apart from them in ability and quality. You remember their revealing question to him after failing to cure the epileptic boy (Mark 9) – *Why could not we cast it out?*

This is the crux of the matter. There is no need for the real leader to be standoffish, because he already stands apart by what he can do and on account of what he is. A leader who practices standoffishness, however excusable, is really demonstrating his own unsureness of his own qualifications for leadership. But standing apart – that is another matter – he must or he is no leader and he must accept the stand-apartness as the price of leadership. It is what is expected of him. It was partly because he *already* possessed it that he was chosen to be the leader. When he recognizes this he can be natural, he can be himself. He can say to himself. *This is my calling, by God's grace I will be what I am*. We could read about this in Romans 12.3ff.

2 *Insincerity*

A second pitfall is insincerity, or playing a part which we think is expected. I first became aware of this in the years shortly after the war. There stood at the bottom of our garden a house where lived an MP of one of the northern constituencies. Normally he drove an impressive Jaguar car, but when he visited his working-class electors he left the car some thirty miles short of the place and continued the journey by bus if not by bicycle. I confess this insincerity turned me off.

I cannot conceive of any church leaders playing this part but there is a pitfall of this nature waiting to trap the unwary. It arises from the commendable expectation that the Christian leader will love his people. We display quite a bit of loving these days in the new eucharistic rites. The leader cannot be expected to show less. So terms of affection are incorporated into semi-official correspondence that would have startled even our immediate forbears. Sometimes they would have been right to be startled. Granted coldness can drive people away and affection is heart warming. But the leader needs to be careful. What are we to think when a secretary, having 'taken down' an affectionate letter, is asked the Christian name of the intended recipient? It is easy to employ terms of endearment because this is the thing to do today. But, if there is no feeling behind the language, the time will come when the insincerity will shine through. Playing a part is a pitfall for leadership, and artificial affection, because it is thought to be proper for a Christian, repels in the long run. Then the leadership suffers. Better to be modest with affection. Few charges are more damaging to leadership than insincerity.

3 Respect of persons

A third pitfall is not easy to label with a word, but it is a form of respecting persons. What I have in mind is the habit (it becomes a habit) of the leader who has time only for *useful* people. Once again, this is understandable if not excusable because it is the function of a leader to spot talent in those he leads and to encourage it. I would be prepared to express this more forcibly. The church leader is not where he is first of all to work out great schemes of his own by which he thinks the mission of God will be forwarded in the world, but to have eyes and ears open for those places and those people where the

Spirit of God is obviously *already* at work, and to lend his support there. It really is a mark of failure on the part of leadership, if some man or some woman of undoubted spiritual ability is left unused for the benefit of the whole Church. Of course there are difficulties, but the general principle stands.

This being so it is not surprising that the leader can fall into the trap of having no eyes, no ears, for the dull, the ordinary and the undistinguished. Some of us have undergone the experience of being at a party and being introduced to someone of standing. He speaks to us, he certainly speaks, but all the time he is looking over our shoulders for someone more important. This then is the pitfall for leaders that they have no time for those at the bottom who will never be more than mediocre. It is true the bottom lot can be boring and awful time-wasters, they do not even have the distinction of doing something frightful. They simply belong to the ninety and nine which need no repentence. It is understandable how the leader can forget all about them, but is it excusable?

4 *Cynicism*

A fourth pitfall is cynicism. This is caused by the necessity for a leader not to accept situations, or even people, at their face value. People make up to leaders. The leader therefore will be wise to sound out opinions of those who do *not* occupy top positions, as a check on his own judgements. The opinion of secretaries are worth noting here. Nevertheless, however great the care exercised, mistakes will be made over situations and over persons. The longer the service in leadership the longer the once short list of 'let downs' becomes. Added to this is the inevitable fact that not only are the successes brought to the attention of the leader but so are the failures, and these latter he will probably have to handle himself. Even clergy break down at times, some lamentably. It is not surprising in the face of all this that the leader long in office becomes somewhat cynical, or if a kinder word be preferred – 'realist'. Who has not seen a leader who began almost starry-eyed come to the point of automatically looking every gift horse in the mouth?

133

So the comment about someone, 'Yes, that is what he/she says but . . .'.

A cynic is not an insensitive person, quite the reverse. He is the sensitive man who has been hurt so deeply he cannot endure any more. So he no longer engages his feelings with anyone or anything. This is not the standoffishness of pride but the shrinking from yet more pain. He would like to commit himself, but not again.

The fact remains, however, cynicism does spoil leadership. It spoils it because it fails to provide encouragement anymore. So enthusiasm gets killed; and enterprise, ruinous for the young, follows. What needs to be remembered in the Christian ministry is that to inoculate the self from being hurt is impossible. There is no way round the back of the cross. But who of us is not tempted to try and find that way?

5 *Three more pitfalls*

I have three more pitfalls in my list, but I will touch on them only very briefly. You will see that the number adds up to seven. I was tempted to set them out under the title, 'The seven deadly sins for leaders', but that would be overdoing it. They hardly qualify for the title sins, for they are really positions into which we slide almost unwittingly.

Anyway here are my three additions.

First *indefiniteness*. I have in mind the sort of leader who invariably gives the answer 'Yes and no' to every question. At its lowest level it represents playing for safety, at its highest the wish not to exclude anyone or any opinion unnecessarily. What it looks like, however, to the led is sitting on the fence, which is singularly uninspiring. People prefer definiteness; they will follow the strong leader. To please everyone is impossible and this is painful for the leader who longs to keep the led together. Hard decisions however are necessary and some opposition inevitable.

Next *professional jealousy*. In every leader there has to be an element of individualism, for without it he would be no leader. Observe a meeting of leaders together and you will see how they are an assembly of unlikes. Each prefers to go his own way. So professional jealousy arises. Here it is necessary to remember that humility does not mean denying individual gifts. What it does mean is recognizing that others also possess distinctive gifts, perhaps the same, perhaps more impressive. Leaders have to accept this about other leaders and not be jealous.

Lastly *self-sufficiency*. That this is a trap for leaders should occasion no surprise. They were chosen for their ability to stand on their own feet. What this can lead to however is an *unawareness* of how dependent they actually are on the other people. There is the family. I can think of a leader, normally composed, almost beside himself because his wife was taken ill. I can think of a ministry seriously impaired because there was no longer any family to support, as once there was. And there are people in the office, helpers a long way down the list in terms of seniority who may be taken for granted, but on their loyalty the leader depends. None of us is really self-sufficient and it is good that from time to time we should recognize this, and maybe this devotional occasion provides an opportunity.

With all these pitfalls who is sufficient for leadership? Who indeed? But as St Paul expressed it, *Our sufficiency is of God*. So, although self examination may be a proper starting point, it cannot properly be the end point. This is why we must go on to look away and out from ourselves, which is what we shall begin to do in the next session.

2 An inspiring leader

We turn now to look outwards in our meditations on leadership and only look inwards in so far as this is suggested by the *object* of our study. That object is the leadership with which David inspired Israel as king, his reign being counted for all time as a golden age, even colouring ideas of Messiahship.

It is worth noting as a preliminary that Samuel, representing the prophetic line, did not wish Israel to possess a king. Their longing was counted an affront against the kingship of Jahweh, the God of Israel, and an affront against Samuel his prophet. But God 'gave them their desire' even if he did 'send leanness withal into their souls' because their first king, Saul, proved to be a failure, lacking spirituality. David his successor was a glorious success. All of which, being interpreted, means that even if we make wrong choices God can, and may, bring good out of it beyond anything we could either desire or deserve; or as St Paul put it, *Where sin did abound, grace did much more abound.*

1 *A combination of contrasting attributes*

David proved to be a brilliant leader. Humble in origin, he was nevertheless quickly marked out as a young man with gifts. No man can rise to be a leader without gifts. Of David it is recorded that he was 'goodly to look upon', special mention being made of his hair and his eyes (1 Samuel 16.12). Attractive to women (Saul's daughter fell in love with him at sight) his manliness was also attractive to men, hence the friendship with Saul's son, Jonathan. So David possessed contrasting qualities. On the one hand there was his poetic nature, and on the other his martial qualities. Of course we do not know how many of the Psalms David wrote, but he can scarcely have had a hand in none. There is, after all, his lament over Saul and Jonathan slain on the field of battle, to bear witness to his haunting literary skill. And since Psalms were meant to be sung, David must have possessed musical skills as well.

In a surprising book to come from the pen of Duff Cooper called *David*, (Rupert Hart-Davis, 1955), there is an arresting picture of David as a young shepherd, entertaining other shepherds at various watering places for the sheep with singing his own songs and accompanying them on a musical instrument he had made with his own hands. No wonder these skills coupled with manly daring soon set him in a class by himself. So David comes before us in the Bible as a man with contrasting attributes. 1 Samuel 16.18 lists these, *cunning in playing the harp, a mighty man of valour, a man of war, prudent in speech and a comely person* – almost a renaissance ideal. This makes for leadership. It makes for leadership because the variety of gifts makes an appeal to diverse groups of people. No one-track mind, no genius (please note), not any *single* gifted man can succeed as a leader of the people. This means that a leader may be surpassed by some subordinate in this or that qualification, and that subordinate in the team still be *unqualified* to take on the leadership. If you are looking for a leader you must look at your candidate *as a whole* and at his/her combination of abilities.

2 *Perfected skills*

Leaders must have gifts, but beware of men and women with gifts alone, if this is all they have. Far from leading people they may trouble people. Not that gifted men and women are not required. Nor can it be thought that piety will make up for the lack of gifts. It will not. More is required, and this David exhibited.

In his youth he possessed supreme confidence in his other skills which he had taken the trouble to perfect. However much Saul might disparage the youthful David facing the experienced giant Goliath of Gath, David knew what he could do with a sling and a stone. He had been experimenting for years, up against lions and bears. He had so mastered his technique that he had every reason to be confident. Gifts, yes, a leader must possess gifts, but he must also have slaved to perfect his skills. There is no short cut to first-class accomplishment.

3 *Astuteness*

I have said that no man rises to a position of leadership by goodness alone. David did not. With him there was astuteness and there was caution, there was patience and there was energy. If, as seemed probable, the throne would one day come to him, he did nothing to hinder it. When Saul was slain on the field of battle David joined in the lament, which is not to say it was not genuine. But he was astute enough not to

137

appear as one ready to bring about a *coup d'état*. As a potential leader David was careful about public opinion.

Then cautious David knew all about *'tout vient à point à qui sait attendre'* – everything comes to him who knows how to wait for it. So when he had Saul in his grasp and could have killed him, and was advised so to do, he waited. Was it not Bismark, of all people, who said that the real statesman waits on events, he does not force them? Put into what some people would write off as pious language – David believed that, if God willed that he should become leader, he would so organize events that the leadership would come his way without him dirtying his hands prematurely to grasp it.

The time came for action and David acted energetically. The Philistines, on seeing Saul's dead body, bestirred themselves to squeeze out David as a possible rival. They failed. David fled to the mountains where he learned the tactics of guerilla warfare. They were hard times. But when his chance came he took it. It required daring but David was no man to shrink from it. He would take the supposedly impregnable fortress of Jebus, and he did. I guess the assault was over in a matter of minutes. And now you can't be a Christian or a Jew or a Moslem without taking that place into your reckoning. We even sing about building Jerusalem (the old Jebus) in England's green and pleasant land. All this was the achievement of David.

4 *Spiritual awareness*

David was astute. He saw the potential importance of Jebus (Jerusalem) as a central place of worship, but could not bring it about. He even felt God was blocking his plan, but such was the spiritual sensitivity of the man that, when he understood this, he accepted the setback as somehow within the providence of God.

Is this a sign of David's greatness as a leader, a willingness to accept without resentment or revenge closed doors to his schemes? No tyrant, we can be sure, understands the importance of submission to the will of God. That David did understand marks him out as a leader in no way partaking of the tyrannical. David was a leader *under God*. I think this scripture is seeking to tell us by this story that leadership is only safe when it is recognized as a divine endowment and therefore is responsible to God. A leader for all his gifts, for all his skills, for all his astuteness, can only successfully accomplish what God knows he can accomplish. This feeling after the hand of God in human destiny was what made David the inspiring leader he was. It is a mark of spiritual mindedness. He had it in his youth and he did not (as is all too common) lose it when he became a leader. This is the key to David. This is why the scriptures call him a man 'after God's own heart'. For all his faults and all his failures, David *wished* to do God's will even when it was contrary to his own schemes. And is it not true that what justifies or condemns us in the sight of God is not what we achieve, but what in our heart of hearts we would like to achieve?

5 *Implications*

And yet, for all his heart, all his head and all the lofty heights which drew people to him, David fell from eminence. He fell through the crude instincts in that human nature we all possess. We should not be proper men and women if we lacked these instincts, but the men and women of God faithful to the end are those same proper men and women who have disciplined and mastered their crude instincts; and so long as they are mastered they become a driving force. If, however, the disciplines fail, the instincts will drive on to fatal consequences, and spirituality will not prevent the inevitable catastrophe.

The implication here is that raw instincts and refined spirituality will probably co-exist in any outstanding leader, and the fact should not surprise us. We should not be surprised that David was attracted by Bathsheba, he would be less of a man if he were not. The sadness is that he lost the mastery of himself. A fall of this kind does not mean a man is bad all through. Sometimes leaders who are responsible for clergymen have to come to terms with this fact about people. Nevertheless, moral standards have to be maintained, and

spirituality is no substitute for them. Neither is morality the
same as spirituality. A moral man, such as Saul, may have no
sense of the hand of God in his life and a spiritually-minded
man like David, who possessed that sense to a marked degree,
may have quite a struggle not to be caught off balance on
account of the powerful instincts operating within his powerful
personality. Conventional religion, so easy to despise, has a
part to play here. It reinforces the discipline of the individual
and so indirectly promotes the possibility of spirituality.

So in the case of David we see a leader caught by a woman
who may have laid a trap for him (I incline to this view, for I
see how masterful Bathsheba was). Be it so or not, his story
runs down to a sorry end. A wretched home life, a divided
family, a kingdom torn by rebellion, with acts of cruelty and
acts of magnanimity all mixed up together. And the last we see
of David is, as an old man in a court riddled with intrigue,
cuddled by a Shunemite girl brought in to do her work.

So the brightest star in Israel's history, from whom even
Jesus took the title 'Son of David', passes off the record sound-
ing this warning at the end, that no leader for all his greatness
is released from the common laws of morality. What a man is
in public and what he is in private cannot be divorced from
each other. Leadership resides in the whole man, not in the
public part of him. There is no safety if this is forgotten.

PRAYER

> *We in part our weakness know,*
> *And in part discern our foe;*
> *Well for us, before thine eyes*
> *All our danger open lies;*
> *Turn not from us, while we plead*
> *Thy compassion and our need.*
>
> *Fain would we thy word embrace,*
> *Live each moment on they grace,*
> *All our selves to thee consign,*
> *Fold up all our wills in thine,*
> *Think and speak and do and be*
> *Simply that which pleases thee.*   *(W. Bright)*

3 The ideal leader

In our last meditation we were thinking of King David as a leader, his strengths and his weaknesses. All the leaders whom Israel experienced exhibited weaknesses. There was no leader without weakness. With some the weakness stood out in greater prominence than the strength. But is there never to be a leader without repelling parts? Is there never to be a perfect leader? This was the question forced out of the disappointments of Israel's more sensitive and reflective people. And if the hurting conclusion has to be that such is not possible, humanly speaking, for the human material out of which all human leaders are fashioned has a basic flaw in it, then is it not possible to project on to the imagination what some ideal leader, say God's acknowledged leader, might be like?

Someone about the time of the Babylonian exile of the Hebrew people thought it was possible. Such an ideal leader would be God's servant. So in four passages of scripture in Deutero-Isaiah (chapters 40–55 of Isaiah) there are set out what are commonly called the four Servant Songs. I know of course that many learned works have been written about the identity of this servant. I do not think a firm answer is possible, because the identity was unclear in the mind of the writer. At one time the servant was reckoned to be all Israel or part of Israel. At another time an historical figure such as Cyrus. But when both Israel and individual saviours failed, the writer's mind was driven out to the conviction that God could not finally fail his people in providing the leader they needed. So he delineated that ideal leader in the four so-called Servant Songs. They stand as isolated pieces though embedded in the general text. They are isolated in another way. There is no reference to them anywhere in the Old Testament. The fact would seem to be that in the Old Testament times no one understood them. Perhaps they cannot be understood until the light of the life of Jesus of Nazareth shines upon them. This is what we Christians believe. But if Jesus filled out these pictures, he did not exhaust them. They provide a pattern for all who have been called to some form of leadership in the congregation of God's people. This is my apology for drawing your attention to them today.

1 *The leader's bearing*

First we are shown what is the bearing of the ideal servant. It is *gentle*. So the first Servant Song reads:

> *He will not call out or lift his voice high,*
> *or make himself be heard in the open street.*

and to this modesty in speaking there is added gentleness in his way of working:

> *He will not break a bruised reed,*
> *or snuff out a smouldering wick.*

In the ideal leader there is no strident 'speechifying', no screaming oratory so common with dictators. Neither does he reckon his model to be found in the saying, 'If you are to make omelets you must break eggs'. This leader is like a man thatching a roof who finds a bruised reed to hand. He does not break it or toss it away, somehow he incorporates it in his building. Nor, if the smoking flame or a lamp calls for snuffing out, does he do so. Rather he cups his hand round it to nurse the spluttering, smouldering spark into a light-giving flame. Gentle in voice then, gentle in manner, such is the bearing of God's ideal leader. On him the Spirit of God rests, and because this is so, he is successful, he makes *justice shine in every race, never faltering, never breaking down*. All this can be read in Isaiah 42.1–4.

2 *The leader's equipment*

And now the leader's equipment. It is surprising. The only weapon he wields is words, but in his mouth they operate as a weapon, even as a sharp sword, or a polished arrow. Listen to this second Servant Song. In it the leader speaks for himself.

> *'Listen to me, you coasts and islands,*
> *pay heed you people far away:*
> *from birth the Lord called me,*
> *He named me from my mother's womb.*

142

He made my tongue his sharp sword
and concealed me under the cover of his hand;
He made me a polished arrow
and hid me out of sight in his quiver.
He said to me, 'You are my servant,
Israel through whom I shall win glory';
so I rose to honour in the Lord's sight
and my God became my strength.   *(Isaiah 49.1–3)*

Note how this leader refers to his call. He could scarcely express it more strongly. *He named me from my mother's womb.* I doubt if any strength of the first magnitude operates with any leader, certainly not a Christian leader, in default of a recognition of a call. We might with profit pause here for a moment and ask ourselves how it is that we find ourselves here today. I do not mean the conference by itself, but how is it that you are here today in the capacity of a leader? Did you angle for your position? Did you 'work it'? Did you arrange it? What *catena* of events then led up to it? How is it that you are now an authorized leader in the Church of God? Is this what you set out to be, or did it come to you? Let this second Servant Song tell you this – you will only be strong in your leadship so long as you remember that you have been called to it.

And now, the leader's equipment. It is words; words which are effective. So although the ideal leader does not lift his voice high, although he never rants, what he says produces results. No leader can sit lightly to words. He will have to employ them. And he needs to remember that he has been called to employ them as part of his office of leadership. And they are to be like a polished arrow upon which trouble and care has been exercised. 'Any old words' will not do. And every speaker/leader of this class has behind him a hidden life. 'He hid me under the cover of his hand' is how the Servant Song puts it. There have to be periods of withdrawal in the leader's life. Too much activity debilitates. Too much church speech, I regret to say, is unconvincing. It comes 'off the cuff', not from the hidden place with God. And sometimes the hidden place with God is entered through the narrow gateway of personal sorrow, but there the arrows, the instrument of the leader's ministry, get polished. I believe this.

3 The leader's experience

And now we begin to walk on a different kind of terrain. The first two Servant Songs could easily be applied to ourselves in so far as we are leaders. With the third Servant Song it is not so easy, and with the fourth Servant Song it will be virtually impossible, though perhaps not entirely.

The third song tells of experience. *The Lord God has given me the tongue of the teacher*. A teaching ministry is what the contemporary Church desperately needs to acquire, for its lack is leading to serious consequences. But what is in mind here is not academic learning, valuable as it is for fashioning tools, but teaching which meets people's needs where they are. Here it is called *skill to console the weary*. This kind of teaching develops from listening. *He sharpened my hearing that I might listen like one who is taught*. Every leader must have his ear to the ground. He must hear what people are saying. Too often answers are given in public speech to questions which the public is not asking. Listening requires effort. The word used for being 'taught' here carries the meaning of chastisement. Learning can be a painful business, but leaders must not shrink from it. Otherwise they will never be effective teachers or leaders. There must be a hard school at the back of them, and experience of toughness and of hard times. The leaders from a narrow background and from a milieu where all was sweetness and light will not stay the course. So don't choose your leader too young. Elevate men and women of experience, experience of the rough.

And now the Servant Song moves on to terrain which belongs to him who is known as the Suffering Servant. But some suffering, even more than that of the pain of the learning process, must be expected. A leader occupies the 'hot seat'. In some sense he can 'never win'. Some there will be who will never be satisfied with his leadership. They will always complain. And jealousy will operate in carping criticism and ostracism. The leader must be prepared. He needs to acquire a certain toughness. *Take your share of hardship, like a good soldier of Jesus Christ*, was what Timothy read in the letter addressed to him as a leader (2 Timothy 2.3). So the third Servant Song:

> *I offered my back to the lash.*
> *and let my beard be plucked from my chin,*
> *I did not hide my face from spitting and insult;*
> *but the Lord God stands by to help me;*
> *therefore no insult can wound me.   (Isaiah 50.6–7)*

What is this? *Athanasius contra mundum?* If you like. Certainly a wholesome imperturbability grounded in 'the certainty of the Lord's sustaining presence'.

4 *The suffering leader*

And now we come to the fourth Servant Song, so well-known I need not read it – Isaiah, chapter 53. Here the theme is suffering for others. It is a suffering which is redemptive in a way ours can never be, though we may perhaps touch on it. A leader for instance must suffer a measure of loneliness. Whatever advice is given to him, in the end it is he alone who has to say 'Yea' or 'Nay'. And he must suffer some misunderstanding. He cannot tell all he knows. So on occasions he will be charged with lack of compassion for the discipline he has exercised. At times he will have to take what is called 'a strong line'. For sensitive leaders this is agonizing. I have known leaders all but broken in health because of this. And there is suffering from long hours of work and the difficulty this causes through isolation from the family.

What are we to say to all this? What are we to say to the leader? Grin and bear it? This fourth Servant Song says, you are *suffering for those you lead*. This is how you partake of the great principle of redemptive suffering which the ideal leader bears. In a sense it is vicarious. It must be borne willingly. The led cannot live without a leader, and the leader cannot lead without suffering. So this suffering contributes to *their life*. This is what he must understand. All this for us Christians has its fulfilment in Christ. We live as his people not simply because he suffered, but because he died under it. And it is in

145

the suffering and the death of him that Christian leaders
minister.

Summary

What are the lessons of these Servant Songs about leadership?
God's leader does not break people with words or deeds.
God's leader is called to minister with the weapon of words
polished and cared for. God's leader operates from the basis of
his own experience, some of it rough. God's leader pays the
price of leadership because he knows that it actually saves
people from chaos and loss. Who would be a leader? Only
he/she who cares about people.

4 The leaders' leader

> Hebrews 2.10 (J. B. Phillips) *It was right
> and proper that in bringing many sons to glory,
> God . . . should make the Leader of their salvation
> a Perfect Leader through the fact that he suffered.*

1 *The perfect leader*

This address has to be short because it is part of the Eucharist.
It is about the leader. There is only one. All others are disciples, and this includes bishops, priests and deacons, deacon-
esses, all diocesan officials, all heads of institutions, deans and
headmasters, wardens of hostels and mothers superior. You
name them. Anyone in a position of leadership, all are
included in our thinking on the subject of this address. Their
leader is Christ. He is their leader because he is perfect as a
leader. Sufferings have made him perfect. Because he is perfect all other leaders fall behind him being imperfect.

This point is not being made on general considerations but
on a particular ground namely Hebrews 2.10 of which J. B.
Phillips made an arresting translation. *It was right that in bringing many sons to glory God . . . should make the Leader of their*

146

salvation a Perfect Leader through the fact that he suffered. Note the word translated 'Leader'. It only occurs here and in Hebrews 12.2. It is *archegos* and in classical usage means 'founder' or 'guide'. There is in reality only one leader, and this is Jesus. He is the leaders' leader.

2 *The leader who delivers*

Now, why is there only one leader who is Jesus? Because he alone has accomplished the rescue operation of us all. J. B. Phillips calls him 'the Leader of *salvation*' in line with the Authorized Version, the Revised Version and the Revised Standard Version. The New English Bible uses the word 'deliver'. Jesus is the one who delivers us. For myself, and I know for a number of other students, William Barclay has lit up this scripture as follows – 'An *archegos* is one who blazes the trail for others to follow. . . . Suppose a ship was on the rocks, and suppose the only way to rescue was for someone to swim ashore with a line in order that, once the line was secured, others might follow. The one who was first to swim ashore would be the *archegos* of the safety of the others. That is what the writer of the Hebrews means when he says that Jesus is the *archegos* of our salvation.' (*The Letter to the Hebrews*, St Andrew's Press, p. 19)

This rescue operation, this leadership in the deliverance operation, was carried out by Jesus through suffering. The two usages of the word *archegos* are both set in a context which mentions this. The reference is to the cross. It is because he delivered us there that he is the leader in a sense that no one else can be. He is therefore the leaders' leader, for they too have been rescued by him.

And they have also been called by him. In our thinking some emphasis has been placed on the necessity for a leader to possess a sense of call if he is to be strong as a leader. Let us not forget the strangeness of this situation or even grow used to it. Normally disciples choose their teacher. Students decide to study under this or that professor. So in the rabbinical schools in Jerusalem pupils chose their rabbi. He could be Hillel or Shammai. But the apostles did not choose Jesus.

147

Quite the reverse. He chose them. Having assured them and chosen them to be disciples, he trained them to be leaders. Thus, those of us who are leaders have a leader ourselves. Our leadership is only safe as we remember this.

3 *The leader in faith*

Jesus is the leaders' leader in another sense than being their deliverer, rescuer or to use the old word – saviour. He is the leader in faith. I refer now to the second usage of the word *archegos*, namely Hebrews 12.2, *Looking unto Jesus the pioneer* (i.e. *archegos*) *and perfecter of faith*. (I am following the Greek text closely here). The point is, no one had faith like Jesus. He blazed a trail in the exercise of faith. He was a pioneer in faith. He went ahead of everybody in the activity of living by faith in the love and power of God available to us all. There never has been anyone like him in this. His trust was absolute, so perfect and so finished that he could remove mountains. This is what the miracles are in the gospel records, examples of mountain moving. They are the outcome of his perfected trust as a man in the heavenly Father. They show what a leader who commits his way to God unreservedly can accomplish.

I know this takes some believing. It always has taken some believing, but it won't go away. At least we know this. Leaders know it only too well. Mountains of difficulty stand in their path that need to be moved. Can they be moved? Is it ever conceivable, let alone possible?

Perhaps it is a pity that nowadays we do not read biographies about such people as George Müller of Bristol, and if we do come across them we write them off as religious cranks. But George Müller has a considerable entry in the *Oxford Dictionary of the Christian Church* (Cross, 2nd edition, OUP).

Müller was born in 1805, in Halberstadt in Germany, and intended for the ministry. As a profligate student at Halle he was suddenly and soundly converted through meeting a group of earnest Christians. As a result he devoted himself to self-denying religious work. In 1829 he came to London to take an appointment with the Society for Promoting Christianity among the Jews but removed to Teignmouth on account of ill-health. There he joined the Plymouth Brethren and became a preacher to the local community. Refusing any kind of salary he decided to live entirely by faith. Two years later he went to Bristol and devoted his whole life to the care of orphan children. Starting with a handful he eventually came to care for two thousand, accommodated in large houses at Ashley Down near Bristol. The whole enterprise was supported entirely by voluntary gifts, the response of prayer and faith.

It is an extraordinary story and leaves most of us standing and wondering if we know anything ourselves about the exercise of faith at all. We have very little experience in our religious life of mountains being moved. But Jesus is our file-leader, our *archegos* in faith and we are called to follow him. What might not our leadership in our sphere of operation achieve if we not only attempted great things for God but actually in faith expected them? Would not mountains be moved?

Which of us who are leaders can rise to this leadership? Which indeed?